T0400329

G8A

and

Contrast

Cohesion

The expansion of an architectural practice from Switzerland to Vietnam, and specifically from Geneva to Hanoi, is an unlikely career move. Not relocation so much as dislocation.

Chaotic, vivacious, and freewheeling Hanoi could be regarded as the anti-Geneva, as the antithesis of the discreet, the manicured, and the buttoned-down.

Yet over the last decade, G8A has oscillated between the prim and proper and the wild and wonderful, retaining a thoroughly Swiss sense of propriety whilst engaging with the bewildering complexities and contradictions of contemporary Asia.

Several of G8A's key projects have been located in Singapore, which is something of a cultural halfway house and often referred to as a tropical Switzerland. Singapore's heat is merciless, and the conditions demand an architecture with a diametrically dissimilar structural approach than that required for a cold climate.

Both culturally and architecturally, G8A has not acquiesced to preconceived notions of irreconcilable contrasts. The team has instead connected and conjoined, and has adapted and assimilated. G8A has maintained a thematic continuity, which has resulted in a cohesion: one that can be formally deciphered in terms of architecture and construction, and perhaps more pertinently, in terms of society and sustainability.

This book presents the architecture of G8A in the seemingly paradoxical context of contrast and cohesion. A series of contrasts, or dualities, or apparent paradoxes, are utilised to explain the processes and observations that have informed the work of G8A. Some of the dualities are new and some are old, and they all interconnect and overlap.

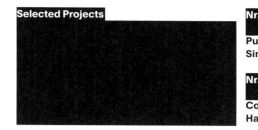

Selected Projects

Vietnam

Punggol Waterway Terraces

Singapore
2009–2015

Punggol Waterway Terraces was a remarkable commission for G8A, and the completed project was also remarkable, both for G8A and for Singapore. G8A had already designed several housing projects in and around Geneva, but they were modest in scale, and only the adjoining Bamboo and Coral apartment blocks (designed in 2007) could be described as having medium density and as categorically urban. Won in an open competition, Punggol Waterway Terraces has an extremely high density — with 1,876 apartments and over 5,000 residents — and it is located in one of Singapore's New Towns, which are effectively cities in themselves. It was a huge leap for G8A, and in many ways, it signified a new approach to public housing in Singapore.

Stretching back to the 1930s, Singapore has had an honourable tradition of innovative public housing, and the zeal with which the New Towns were built, and filled with affordable and extremely liveable apartment blocks, was possibly the most enduring motif of the country's economic transformation after it became an independent state in 1965. The blocks were referred to by the acronym HDB (after the Housing and Development Board), and the first wave of large-scale housing was comprised of elemental yet quietly elegant modernist towers, which relied upon passive energy strategies to shade and cool the residents. Many private apartment towers were also designed with the same intentions, with larger budgets that afforded more in the way of architectural flamboyance. As the advent of widespread air-conditioning removed the need for natural cooling, the HDBs and the private apartments no longer looked tropical, and they were not open to the elements and to each other: they were hermetically sealed, and inevitably, so were their occupants.

At the beginning of the 21st century, Singapore's town planners faced two problems — unsustainable construction and an unsociable lifestyle — which could feasibly be solved simultaneously by reverting to the fundamental architectural principles of the pre-air-conditioning era. G8A's scheme for Punggol, a New Town on the north of the island, conspicuously implemented methods to maximise sun shading and natural cooling, and actively encourages community interaction.

The development comprises two eighteen-storey blocks on either side of a small manmade river, and these two blocks are sheathed in continuous bands of concrete, which project at an angle from the façade to serve as balcony walls for the apartments above and as sun screens for the apartments below. Both blocks have a 'molecular' plan of linked hexagons, whose three-way open-to-the-elements intersections facilitate cross-ventilation throughout the double-loaded corridors and — with the aid of additional voids — through the apartments themselves. The hexagons are sliced open to accommodate extensive landscaped courtyards, which step down to the river, as does the terraced massing of the blocks, inspired by the romantic notion of hillside rice paddies.

The presumed monumentality of such a massive construction has been camouflaged by the landscaping and the tapering profile of the blocks, and virtually obviated by the horizontal striations of the white concrete bands. In fact, a pleasurable and unreservedly natural environment has been created in the contextually neutral tabula rasa of an expanding Asian city. The integration of the luxuriant landscape with the horizontal rhythms of the architecture exudes a poetic harmony, which appears in marked contrast to the isolated orthogonal verticality currently prevalent in large-scale public housing.

The architecture and the planning are genuinely inventive, both in terms of sustainability and sociability, and the project must be now regarded as a serious (and economically viable) prototype for the form of construction that will define and decide the future of Asian cities. Housing the extraordinary amount of residents of those rapidly expanding cities will be an endless challenge, and any tangibly successful solutions will have far-reaching consequences for global sustainability and communal wellbeing.

→ pp. 15, 154, 208

Coalimex

Hanoi, Vietnam
2008–2013

Despite the extraordinary contrasts between the two cities, the Coalimex office building in central Hanoi would not look out of place in G8A's architectural oeuvre in Geneva. The principles and strategies were effortlessly transposed from a cold climate to a hot climate, and from the ordered urbanity of Switzerland to the noise and congestion of Vietnam. The Coalimex building utilises the same *parti* as the Avenue de France project (designed two years earlier), whereby a façade comprised of two layers of glass responds to and then moderates the specific local context. Both buildings have an abstracted yet eye-catching presence and serve as ordering devices within a greater urban scale.

Only two city blocks away from the delightful Hoan Kiem Lake, the Coalimex building is located on a one-way street whose heavy traffic has effectively precluded the footpath sociability that typifies Hanoi. G8A decided to pull the building back from the street, in order to decompress the claustrophobic nature of the precinct and enlarge the footpath, thereby creating some breathing space and some public space, which is sheltered by a glass canopy. The Coalimex project thus continues the street-level social interaction strategies employed by G8A in the Bamboo and Coral projects, designed a year earlier for Geneva. Two vertical layers of glass, set 60 cm apart, rise above the canopy and sheath the entire street façade of the building in order to reduce the noise of the traffic. The outer layer is fritted with a 'mineral' pattern, in recognition of the coal mining company that commissioned the building, and the large glass panels — supported by brackets — are separated by a 5mm joint. The windows of the inner glass wall can be opened for ventilation, and the 60 cm gap between the layers of glazing serves as a thermal chimney, funnelling air up from the base of the building.

Although the Coalimex building appears slender and almost two-dimensional from the street, it has a deceptively large plan and mass. The glass façade screens an eight-storey block with a small footprint, and as this is the only structure that can be seen from street level, it effectively hides a much larger ten-storey masonry block placed to the rear and is accessed through a central light well-cum-lift lobby. The walls of the rear block are 80 cm thick, which means that the windows are deeply recessed to facilitate shading and enable occupant privacy. In order to blend with the tall trees retained at the rear of the site, the deep-set window reveals are painted green, as are the break-out loggia work-spaces on each floor. The *parti* of Coalimex reiterates — in built form — the strategy first proposed by G8A in 2003 for their Green House project in Geneva, whereby the street elevation responded in a deferential, almost ethereal manner to a public precinct, whilst the rear elevation addresses the typical Hanoian proximity of close neighbouring structures.

→ pp. 25, 212

Coral

Geneva, Switzerland
2009–2011

The Coral apartments extend along the north-western side of a cul-de-sac in a tightly built residential area near Geneva's city centre, and form one half of a pair of adjoining blocks designed by G8A that utilise colour and sharply delineated details to overcome the restrictive regulations of the precinct's masterplan. The adjacent Bamboo apartments are distinguished by the random compositions of its bright green glass panels, which slide to screen indoor/outdoor living areas, whilst Coral is notable for the rigour of its metalwork and its pared-back elemental façade.

The masterplan dictated that the apartment block could rise to 21 metres, with two additional recessed levels on the roof, and as no balconies were permitted, the narrow plot size had to be maximised. This confinement led to the creation of public space on the footpath beneath the cantilevered apartments, and the building is overtly orientated towards the life of the street, an urbane and highly convivial avenue delineated by a long grove of trees. Each apartment is focused around a large living room-cum-loggia that looks directly on to the street through two floor-to-ceiling windows, and which can be shaded from morning sunlight by vertically-adjustable canvas blinds, vividly coloured in four shades of magenta and red. The apartments are multi-functional and can be simply reconfigured to suit the requirements of a variety of occupants: office spaces and guest rooms can be screened from the central living area by sliding doors, and the bedrooms were placed at the rear.

As with several contemporaneous G8A buildings, Coral is notable for the appearance of its façade. The street elevation of vertiginous glass, precisely dissected by thin lines of black steel, recalls the austere yet dynamic modernism of Erich Mendelsohn in the 1920s, whilst the decorative details have a hint of Art Nouveau. The steel pilasters, which segment the horizontal expanse of the glass façade, serve as screens for narrow windows in the apartments, as they are perforated by cut outs shaped like coral (hence the name of the apartments). The sliding glass doors of the façade form part of an open/closed and inside/outside program of living space flexibility within each apartment. The architecture of Coral is not just skin-deep, as the external tectonic rigour expresses the internal systems for modular readjustment.

→ pp. 32, 213

The Parks

Quy Nhon, Vietnam
2016

With a long curving beach and a placid estuarine lake, the coastal town of Quy Nhon, some 450 kilometres north of Ho Chi Minh City, is being actively developed as a tourist resort. G8A was asked to submit a proposal for an 'iconic' twin-tower hotel and residential building located at the centre of the beachfront, across the road from the seaside promenade. G8A decided to reinterpret the notion of 'iconic', and prioritised the building's function rather than its form: rather than supplying glass-clad shapely silhouettes, G8A proposed an interlocking structure that would integrate with the beachfront and the town in a highly sociable manner.

The program and the massing have much in common with G8A's Vertical Green City scheme for Hanoi (designed in the same year), which also focuses on horizontal connectivity, both within the building and with the surrounding urban precinct. As with that Hanoi project, G8A resisted implementing the standard template of two single-use towers rising above a self-contained podium, and provided a layered publicly accessible podium surmounted by towers that mixed the residential and hotel components. One hotel was placed on the lower levels of one tower, whilst another was positioned at the top of the other, and one set of apartments occupies each of the towers. The twin towers are linked by two semi-public sky bridges: a lower bridge serves as a garden for the apartment residents, whilst the higher bridge has a pool and bar for the hotel guests. A large tunnel beneath the seafront roadway and a series of landscaped gardens connect the development with the beach and public parks.

The sky bridges also serve to brace the towers, meaning that the structure can be lighter and the cores can be thinner, thus enabling additional porosity: critical for cross-ventilation and for the provision of views. As Quy Nhon is laid out between two hills — a backdrop that has come to symbolise the town — this vision of two slender towers with layers of greenery was crucial to the 'iconic' value of the project. The Parks can be viewed as a fulcrum for the town and its topography, re-affirming a natural sense of place, rather than asserting a man-made intervention. In the event of typhoons and the need for security on non-working days, sliding panels made from polycarbonate can close off the building.

The factory opens out to two large landscaped courtyards, which provide much-needed social and relaxation space in a district that has no parks or public facilities. This courtyard typology is akin to that of the Hoa Lac High-Tech Park, inspired by the notion of a continuous organic matrix of 'villages' for workers, with communal spaces enclosed by low-rise and easily accessible buildings. The planning, as well as the architecture, can thus be viewed as a prototype for moderating tropical conditions in order to create a flexible and convivial working environment, to restore connections with nature, and to dramatically reduce energy consumption.

→ pp. 40, 216

The Birds

Geneva, Switzerland
2007–2008

The wooded parkland known as the Bois de la Bâtie sits on a hillside above the confluence of the Rhone and the Arve in central Geneva. Since 1985, it has been used by the City of Geneva to protect endangered species of birds and animals. When the avian flu epidemic of 2006 threatened several species of migratory birds, G8A was commissioned to design an aviary that would prevent those birds from flying away and contracting the disease, thus potentially ensuring the longevity of those species.

To avoid disturbing any existing woodland, a small lawn near the park's hilltop entrance was selected as the site, and the plan of the aviary was not geometrically derived, as it simply followed the shape of that open space. G8A was anxious not to erect any structure that would be perceived as 'urban', or indeed as a piece of architecture: the architects wanted to reinforce the continuity of the forest with a structure that blended in with the trunks, the branches, and the canopy of leaves. The aviary required two separate enclosures, in order to prevent certain species from intermingling, and the pathway between the cages now forms a graceful gateway to the parklands. The 'blending in' was extremely elemental, as the tubular steel columns simply mimicked the trunks and branches of the trees, and a curvaceous concrete roof slab — only 8 cm thick — forms a delicate canopy. As the colour of the slender columns was matched with the surrounding foliage, the structure is effectively camouflaged within a screen of trees, which allows the concrete canopy to draw attention to itself as a tangible presence, as an amoebic abstraction drifting through the leaves above. To preclude the possibility of the birds breaking out of their cage, the netting had to be strong and tight, and it was fixed directly to the forest floor by hooks embedded in the soil, which eliminated the need for a concrete podium and maintained the ecological continuity.

The architecture of The Birds was non-architecture, the structure was completely unobtrusive, and this approach of 'invisibility' was also used by G8A in several other projects, such as The Dots in Hanoi and the ICRC Visitors' Centre in Geneva.

→ pp. 43, 160, 218

The Bridge

Hanoi, Vietnam
2016–2019

The Bridge embodies a design solution responding to the context of the spatial and socio-economic landscape of urban Vietnam. Housing the teams of the several luxury brands that make up the OpenAsia Group, typologically located between warehouse and logistic service buildings, the structure will stand enigmatically in the middle of Old Hanoi.

The proposal envisioned the office building as a series of platforms lifted by two cores of concrete; one containing the circulation paths and main services, the second being the support for all documentation so called "the memory wall". In-between can be found an open space, free of any columns, open widely on both sides to large windows creating unobstructed panoramic rooms across each floor.

This sensation of space brings forth the particularity of the building, in stark contrast to the surrounding density the platforms open to the environment offering users a rare context of open space. These sweeping office areas represent synergies and transparency, allowing for a maximum of flexibility for any future use.

Here G8A proposes to diverge density with a structural and visual porosity, the doorless entrance of the building seemingly an extension of the sidewalk and the building's north-south exposure permitting an open platform. Facades are placed voluntarily in recess to absorb the potential construction of surrounding buildings, in anticipation of further growth in the coming years.

The mesh net on the entrance side and green façade cabling at the rear of the building provides passive shading and brings a sense of intimacy. In the back of the building, the open vertical space allows the site to generate its own light and ventilation, a soft filter from the nearby chaos.

Upon entering the building, we are met with cues of materiality that embody the Open-Asia philosophy "the transformation of raw material to fine product". A prevailing use of the brut texture of concrete in relation to light hues and fine polished details of bronze, communicates the idea of transforming rough to precious and coarse to polished. This precedes another sense of contrast as the user moves from the defined areas of circulation to the panoramic open work spaces.

Here, G8A applies an adaptation of the "sustainable ruin" philosophy in the urban density of old Hanoi, a concept previously developed in the High-Tech Park of Hao-Lac. The ideology proposes creations of highly adaptable structural system underscoring the robust infrastructural nature of the building. Prioritizing the climatic answer, the spatial relationships, the exoskeleton constructive logic but also a strong identity expression that allows for future adaptation.

→ pp. 48, 147, 220

Bamboo

Geneva, Switzerland
2009–2011

Designed as a twinset for a small precinct tucked away in a busy yet unremarkable suburban neighbourhood near central Geneva, the Bamboo and Coral apartment blocks have a shared urban form and a wilfully dissimilar appearance. The interplay between the two buildings is key to the architecture and to G8A's overall urban strategy. The architectural *parti* for both buildings is avowedly rational and Miesian, with thin lines and clearly articulated elements, but the over-riding desire was for the creation of communal cohesion, individual comfort, and a distinct sense of identity.

The Coral apartments are aligned upon and overlook a short tree-filled cul-de-sac, whilst the Bamboo apartments shoot off at a right angle from the end of the street. According to state regulations, the Bamboo apartments were built for sale, whilst the Coral apartments were to be rented, and as the precinct masterplan prescribed a height of twenty-one metres, both buildings would have seven storeys with provision for another two recessed levels on the roof. Townhouses with their own gardens were placed on the rooftops and clad with alucobond. At the end of the cul-de-sac, the two blocks are separated (or conjoined) by a communal open space, which features a totemic sculpture by Fabrice Gygi as a cheeky commemoration of the twenty-one metre height imposition.

The use of colour is fundamental to G8A's determination to provide an identity — something more than a generic Swiss apartment block — and Bamboo is resplendently clad with arrays of sliding glass panels tinted in four shades of green. On the southwest elevation, the panels can be used to screen the loggias, or outdoor rooms, which extend from large family living areas. These loggias are finished with warm-toned timber, and the resultant harmony with the green panels provides an appearance that might typify a warmer climate and environment.

As it does not adjoin a roadway, Bamboo is relatively secluded, and as it was raised 1.5 metres above ground level, the apartments are reasonably private, but the design was predicated upon a desire to integrate with the neighbourhood. The inside/outside nature of the loggias is immediately construed as a blurred transition zone between public and private, whereby each apartment can be opened out to engage with the sights and sounds of the local community. The block is surrounded by and accessed from playgrounds and gardens, and the fine lines between public, semi-public, and private have not been drawn: a friendly

sociable ambience prevails throughout a clois-
tered neighbourhood.

→ pp. 50, 221

Hanoia House

Hanoi, Vietnam
2016

The Old Quarter of Hanoi, north of Hoan Kiem
Lake, remains one of the most fascinating and
lively precincts to be found anywhere in Asia,
with a maze of streets lined by stalls, cafés,
and small shops. Located on Hang Dao (named
after the silk-sellers who once made this street
their own), the display rooms of the Hanoia
House boutique occupy each of the three volumes of a traditional courtyard house.

The plots of the Old Quarter are very
long and thin, and the houses — referred to as
'tube' houses — are squeezed between party
walls, and often extruded vertically to an alarm-
ing degree. The Hanoia House, however, remains resolutely horizontal and it should also
be contextualised as a shophouse, a typology
that typifies — in various forms — many town
centres throughout Southeast Asia. The Straits
Settlements of Penang, Melaka, and Singapore had colonial era cores comprising rows
of near-identical double-storey shophouses
fronted and shielded by 1.5-metre arcades, a
clear response to the need for protection from
the extreme heat.

Hanoi shophouses, however, have a more
individualistic appearance and planning arrangement, with a sense of enclosure that reflects the immediate context of the neighbourhood and the commercial requirements of the
occupants. The heterogeneous streetscape
of the Old Quarter is not as 'grand' as the band-
ed rows of the Straits Settlements (the French
colonial regime was less prescriptive) and the
Hanoia House has a quaintly demure and reticent appearance. An unadorned yellow-paint-
ed façade — sandwiched between blocks of
taller and dishevelled shopping emporia —

resembles a gateway to a humble temple enclosed beneath a low-pitched tile roof. A small
temple comprised part of the original structure, and it has been retained for Buddhist wor-
shippers in the attic above the entry volume.

Three ground floor showrooms, which
display a range of lacquered artefacts, extend
the length of the ground floor with two small,
sheltered courtyards. Somewhat dwarfed by
high party walls on both sides, the ambience
could have been dank and claustrophobic — ill
suited to such a boutique — but G8A opened
up the spaces to stimulate ventilation and fill
the volumes with daylight. Bricks are used in
the entry and the courtyards in breezeblock
patterns, whilst sheer glass doors and crafted joinery establish a local sense of place:
both contemporary and traditional at once.

The Asian shophouse typology, where
light-wells and courtyards are juxtaposed
with living and working spaces to form a continuous inside/outside volume, has informed
much of the interior planning of much of G8A's
recent work. The architects' understanding of
Hanoi's urbanity has been synthesised with
their research into the traditional rural houses of northern Vietnam, which form communi-
ties linked by semi-public spaces. The organic external arrangements of the rural houses
have been transposed at a larger scale with
such projects like the Hoa Lac High-Tech Park
and the Jakob Factory, whilst the internal working spaces are imbued with an awareness of
the attributes of the shophouse and the commercial lineage of pre-modernist Hanoi.

→ pp. 54, 222

Striped Living

Crans-près-Céligny, Switzerland
2007–2012

Located on the main street of a quiet hillside
village north of Geneva, the Striped Living development provides an architectural and social solution to a very Swiss dilemma. Land is a
precious commodity in Switzerland, but many
of its more affluent citizens are not enthusias-
tic about relinquishing their rights to a private
house. This means that satisfying the demands
of the homeowner is not always compatible
with the local building regulations or with the
over-riding requirement to minimise the country's construction footprint.

The Striped Living townhouses were designed for a clientele that expects a degree of
luxury, but as with the nearby La Tuilerie and
the Red Houses developments, G8A's masterplan provided a mutually acceptable alterna-
tive to the construction of individual villas.
Although appearing as single villas from the
exterior, each of the four-storey blocks contains six units that are occupied as if they were
stand-alone houses. Kept apart by a light-filled
corridor and a staircase well, the townhouses
do not have communal walls, and they effec-

tively have four façades. As fifty-two town-houses will eventually be built, this strategy means that the scale of the village and the adjoining farmland will not be disrupted by the unwelcome and unsustainable intrusion of too many detached villas. And, as a benefit ensuing from this medium-density approach to private housing, the courtyards and gardens surrounding the townhouses are public spaces, which have become an integral part of the village's streetscape.

G8A's intention to balance sociability with efficiency is refreshing when seen in the context of a Swiss village, where self-contained box-like villas have proliferated as a result of rigid planning regulations and what might be described as a selfish mindset. Such a community-minded approach has been intrinsic to the work of G8A in Asia, and the cluster of Striped Living townhouses specifically encourages social interaction whilst heeding the requirements for sustainable construction.

G8A was the architectural practice for two of the first five blocks built, and any subsequent construction must conform with the building envelope and staggered site plan stipulated by G8A. As a divergence from the assumed responsibility to contextualise, each of the townhouse villas has a flat roof (as opposed to the prevalent pitched roofs), but as the scale of the development harmonises with the existing village and as the new buildings are set back from the street, this modernist gesture bestows subtle variety to the character of the village. Each of the blocks, which can be seen in the round, has a plan that encourages the recession and protrusion of volumes, and in order to maintain privacy for the residents, every façade must be clad with vertical fins. G8A exploited both of these (self-imposed) requirements with their pair of townhouses to produce a sculpted three-dimensional composition, animated by the rippling surfaces of the slender fins. When the fins are viewed obliquely, the buildings appear as a solid mass, but when seen in elevation, they are little more than fine vertical striations, exposing the porosity of the structure. The original intention was to clad the buildings with wooden battens, but travertine was used instead, which although more expensive, guaranteed that no maintenance would be required and that the townhouses would have a discreetly intrigued identity. Establishing an identity, through the selection of materials or the use of colour, has been a recurring theme in G8A's urban, and semi-urban projects.

→ pp. 56, 150, 224

Hoa Lac
High-Tech Park

Hanoi, Vietnam
2010–2015

The Hoa Lac High-Tech Park will form an integral component of a satellite town development to the west of Hanoi, and G8A was commissioned to provide an overall masterplan for a site larger than 85 hectares, which forms part of what is envisaged as the Silicon Valley of north Vietnam. The Hoa Lac area is currently flat, rural scrubland, dotted with small villages and farms, notable for its red soil, and overlooked by the foothills of the mountain ranges that enclose the Hanoi Basin. Despite the overriding imperative to convert the peaceful backwater into a money-pumping extension of the prescribed mega-city, G8A's masterplan strove to emulate the existing rural typology by treating each campus of the high-tech park as a communal village centred around courtyards. The campuses, which will have between 3,000 and 8,000 workers, will be linked with one another as a series of low-scale techno-villages, clustered as a sub-urban progression along the shorelines of the small lakes of the Hoa Lac plain.

G8A was indeed fortunate to have been given a site that already possessed one of the favoured ingredients for a new town — a landscape replete with intimate waterways and lakes — and they readily appropriated this topography, not just for the masterplan but for the forms of the individual buildings. Each high-tech campus comprises blocks with a variety of trapezoidal plans, thus responding to the natural irregularities of the watercourses on the site. The plan of each building, each campus, and the entire high-tech park, is predicated upon the notion of semi-public space, exactly as in a local village, whereby each worker (or resident) can sociably interact with their immediate co-inhabitants and with those from adjoining campuses. The circulation routes through each campus are not air-conditioned, and workers are encouraged to use the stairs in the buildings, which will be no higher than four storeys.

Three initial buildings — High-Tech Landscape (2011–2013), The Dots (2013–2014), and Concrete Lace (2014–2017) — have been completed and a fourth is currently under construction. High-Tech Landscape and The Dots are essentially two halves of a discrete entity: the former comprises a three-storey office block with an E-plan, which embraces the latter, a low-slung single storey pavilion containing an alfresco cafeteria. The passageways that flow through The Dots perform as the entry from an inland road to a landscaped courtyard between the two buildings. High-Tech Landscape overlooks a lake to the south with a green-coloured façade reminiscent of G8A's Bamboo apartments in Geneva, whilst the northern courtyard façades — recessed on the E-plan — are adorned with pivoting vertical timber shutters.

The Dots cafeteria is a humble yet expressive structure, which on the one hand represents a continuation of G8A's 'architecture of disappearance', and on the other offers an interpretation of traditional Vietnamese communal houses. The 'architecture of disappearance' had been established by several Geneva projects, most notably The Birds aviary, where the façade is almost invisible, the structure is unobtrusive, and the roof is little more than a thin horizontal line. In traditional Vietnamese architecture, the brick-paved 'bia dinh' courtyards were enclosed by pavilions that were open to the elements with a structure solely comprised of columns and roof. The Dots performs as a highly convivial update on the principle of the 'bia dinh', with three circular bamboo gardens admitting daylight and extending the greenery on the roof to the cafeteria below. The roof of The Dots is a particularly intriguing space, as its lushly planted ground-plane is calculatedly difficult to discern, thus performing as a highly effective device to merge and mingle the landscape and the buildings of the campus.

→ pp. 60, 159, 224

Avenue de France

Geneva, Switzerland
2009–2012

Originally commissioned by the World Trade Organisation, the Avenue de France building was G8A's first project for one of the many such Geneva-based international organisations, and several more were to follow. Its architecture was rational and precise, but the success of the design resulted from its clearly delineated awareness of contextual transition, from its role as a public edifice, and from its distinctively personalised identity. These qualities were to continually reappear in G8A projects, both in Switzerland and Asia.

The urban form and the material detailing for the office block were determined by its prominent, yet exposed location, which presented one specific problem and one marvellous opportunity. Designed as an L-shaped plan, the building directly adjoins and overlooks the vast agglomeration of railway tracks adjacent to Geneva's main station, and occupation would be impossible without total soundproofing from the screeching and clanking of the trains, and from traffic noise on the Avenue de France. The site also marked a demarcation line between the boisterous downtown ambience of the lakeside Les Paquis district and the manicured gentility of the international organisations headquartered on the hillside above. The architecture was both a response to the need for aural insulation and to the building's conspicuous position in Geneva's cityscape, and these two considerations were simultaneously resolved by the design of the façade.

The external elevations are distinguished by sheer walls of glass, which comprise two layers of multi-coloured, vertical, rectangular panels. The building is thus wrapped within a double skin of glazing: an acoustic buffer with an outer layer that absorbs the initial impact of the railway noise, and an inner layer that definitively obliterates any residual sounds. As the lengthier external elevation faces east over the railways, the tinted glass also modulates the heat and brightness of the morning sun. The building is entered from Avenue de France, and in conjunction with an existing building of the same height, the L-shaped plan facilitated the creation of a semi-public garden courtyard. Notwithstanding the role of its appearance in the context of Geneva's cityscape, the new building was conceived as a continuation of a block of medium-height office buildings, and it tangibly reinforced the scale of its immediate neighbourhood.

The variously hued and highly visible eastern façade stands as an unmistakable representation of the transition point between the wall-to-wall liveliness of the streetscapes in Les Paquis and the architecturally discreet landscape of the international zone to the northwest. The building is a landmark, but it is a quietly assertive and appropriately Genevois landmark. The façade is meticulously assembled, it is colourful yet restrained, and its visual delight ensues from the continuous movements of spangled sunlight and reflected clouds across a shimmering glass mosaic.

→ pp. 68, 226

Concrete Lace

Hanoi, Vietnam
2014–2016

As the third building completed in the first phase of the Hoa Lac High-Tech Park, the Concrete Lace office block is adjacent to High-Tech Landscape and The Dots, connected to those buildings via a short walkway, and sited on the lakefront. The plan is that of an irregular pentagon, with four levels of offices completely enclosing a spacious garden courtyard. G8A took its cue for the Hoa Lac buildings from the local villages, and the courtyard plays the role of the village square. External corridors overlooking the courtyard serve as circulation routes — like narrow village streets — and in conjunction with large breezeways carved out of the building's mass, diminish any sense of enclosure (or claustrophobia) within the compound.

The most striking architectonic features are the groupings of crooked columns that 'march' across the external and internal façades: a melodic abstraction kept in check by the equally prominent horizontal lines of the protruding floor slabs. This structural strategy has delivered twin benefits for both the building's developer and its occupants, as the absence of internal columns means that the size and flexibility of the workspace areas has been maximised, whilst the thick columns and extended floor slabs provide insulation and sun-shading. The building has now turned green — on both the external and internal elevations — as abundant vines and creepers have flourished on a network of cables attached to the columns and floor slabs. The greenery grows skywards whilst stretching out to weave into the surrounding landscape.

G8A describes the structural strategy as designing a 'sustainable ruin', by which the architects mean that the building's monumental and muscular exoskeleton cannot be tampered with by any subsequent accretions, extensions, or alterations. The concrete superstructure will remain in situ as a passive and totally sustainable (no energy required) edifice for all future occupants. When one views the horizontal mass of Concrete Lace, the image of the building is the external structure, not the glazing, or the infill, or indeed the landscaping. The exoskeleton is the body of the building, and any other components are regarded as ephemeral, as modular inserzions, or external wrapping paper.

G8A has factored the realities of 21st century construction and property development into the architectural equation: the architects have acknowledged that the budgets for urban development in rapidly expanding cities will be tightly capped, and that the lifespan of the external cladding will be relatively short. Far better then to build a low-cost, low-maintenance structure with an open-plan interior space, which will also prove to be truly sustainable if and when technology and commercial priorities need to adapt to climate change and an inappropriate use of building materials.

→ pp. 72, 149, 228

The Twin-Lah

Geneva, Switzerland
2016–2019

Looking up towards the Mont-Blanc from Thônex (Geneva, Switzerland) this isn't just a project for a house, it is the narration of a story.

Since the very first sketches, the objective requirements of the client led the narration and the process through which the house was designed. Living at that time in Singapore, one of his main wishes was to bring a piece of his home-town to Switzerland. With the name "The Twin-Lah" G8A winks at the colloquial Singaporean dialect Singlish; a mix of English, Malay, Hokkien, Teochew, Cantonese, and Tamil. And through the warm pigmentation and texture, is evoked traditional Singaporean shop-houses. The design of this residence establishes a dialogue with its surroundings, playing with strong contrast in order to take place within the neighborhood and the community.

As requested by the client this project includes a villa orientated to enhance the view of the Mont-Blanc and a smaller house to be rented. Similar to the "Twin House" project completed ten years prior, G8A integrate rather than duplicate the houses producing a single entity with imperceptible separations.

The garden was to remain as untouched as possible so after discussion the house was finally set, in a radical gesture, directly against the property's boundary. The house was then conceived as a stack of 3 "T" shaped structures, absorbing forces from its surrounding context to articulate in and outdoor spaces.

Designed as a sensitive object that responds to its context and to the personal narrative of its owner, this project appears as the story-telling of a Singaporean pink house conceived, adapted and placed, after careful consideration, at the foot of the Mont-Blanc. These powerful contrasts create architectural challenges that The Twin-Lah balances harmoniously.

→ pp. 78, 229

Green Dots

Seoul, South Korea
2016 Competition Entry

The small tree-filled Nodeul Island in the Han River, which flows through the centre of Seoul, currently serves as little more than a foundation for a road bridge — a circumstance that appears quite anomalous in such a densely populated city — but the site offers an opportunity to create something special. Somewhat surprisingly, rather than erecting an iconic edifice, a decision was made to retain the existing landscape and establish a communal arts and crafts facility, whose occupants could create their individual working 'capsules' within an architecturally designed framework.

G8A proposed a three-dimensional grid of post and beam with platforms, which would spread across the allocated site as a modular steel lattice to support, contain, and cover the variety of individually designed workshops and studios. As the complex would be fully open to the public, the surrounding spaces were just as significant as the enclosed structures, and the new environment aimed to seamlessly integrate the existing trees and grasses with the pared-back components of the framework.

The landscape would be used as an extension of the working spaces, so that the entire community — which would not be residential — has the back-to-nature ambience of a collection of allotments or market gardens. Elemental, participatory, adaptable, and sustainable, the project could be seen as glimmer of environmental and social rehabilitation in the midst of a mega-city.

→ pp. 80, 230

Lola

Geneva, Switzerland
2009–2013

The plan for the Lola apartments, located in southern Geneva, represents an intriguing interpretation of the site's unusual shape and topography. The lozenge-shaped site slopes steeply from a laneway to a small stream edged by tall trees, and a curving terraced block was placed alongside this lane, so that the apartments open out to southern sun, with a view over a steeply pitched lawn to an adjoining forested park. The apartments taper down the northern perimeter, cranking and twisting to follow the contours of the slope in plan and section, and G8A refers to the building's form as that of an 'adaptable caterpillar'.

Clad with a skin made from strips of larch wood, the apartment block does indeed have a sinuous, snake-like presence, and in the manner also used by G8A in the Striped Living and La Tuilerie projects, the façade is punctured by an abstracted arrangement of deep-set windows. As with Striped Living and La Tuilerie, a balance was sought between public and private, between sociable and reticent, and between formal and informal. Communal interaction was encouraged (though not prioritised) through a strategy of semi-enclosure in the building mass, and by architectonic deference. The ebbs and flows and the ins and outs of the architecture have purposefully engendered a sense of intimacy and community, as well as an organic integration with the gentle wooded landscape.

Although the development appears as a single edifice, it is actually comprised of a new block at the top of the site, which unites with a refurbished existing building on the slope below. The new structure does not form a solid wall, as each unit is accessed from pathways that lead from the laneway to the common lawn, and the terraces formed by recesses and protrusions in the building's mass are used for balconies and outdoor eating areas. Apartments in the existing building block were designed as duplexes, whilst those in the new block have a central core surrounded by continuous spaces.

G8A's notions of using hybrid forms and circulation routes to stimulate sociability, and to reconcile functional efficiency with a relaxing environment, were relatively easy to implement in such small housing developments. On a much larger scale, however, the *parti* of using a porous mass to partially enclose a semi-public social space was to become a predominant theme in G8A's Asian projects, and is intriguing to note that the contextual disparities between Switzerland and Southeast Asia have not precluded the typological commonalities.

→ pp. 82, 232

Jakob Factory

Ho Chi Minh City, Vietnam
2015–2019

Located in an industrial area of Ho Chi Minh City, the design for a net-making factory was directed by a desire for environmental sustainability, by the provision of social amenity, and by the need for worker well being. The architectural strategy can be viewed as a prototype for successfully implementing a pleasant and naturally ventilated workplace in the hot and sweaty climate of southern Vietnam: there will be no air-conditioning, as the factory will only be cooled by cross-ventilation. The decision to abstain from artificial cooling was not made by the architects alone, as a company survey of its workers revealed that they were not happy with air-conditioning, declaring that their health was suffering.

The production areas of the factory are orientated to receive the prevailing north winds and, in order to optimise the amount of fresh air flowing through the workplace, permeable screens of greenery will substitute for 'traditional' walls of masonry or corrugated iron. Comprised of vines growing from planters, the natural green façades will shade the workers from the morning and afternoon sun, and the foliage will significantly reduce the temperature. As the workplace requires a ceiling height of 4.5 metres to accommodate the tall net-making equipment, a significant degree of ventilation is possible, as it would be in any large community space.

Although the notion of a green screen instead of a solid wall was (in terms of ventilation) a sound idea, one intrinsic problem needed to be resolved: keeping the rain out. In tropical Ho Chi Minh City, heavy downpours are common, and the monsoon season can last for six months. The density of the plantings has thus been calibrated to admit as much cooling breeze as possible whilst preventing ninety percent of the rainfall from entering the factory. In the event of typhoons and the need for security on non-working days, sliding panels made from polycarbonate can close off the building.

The factory opens out to two large landscaped courtyards, which provide much-needed social and relaxation space in a district that has no parks or public facilities. This courtyard typology is akin to that of the Hoa Lac High-Tech Park, inspired by the notion of a continuous organic matrix of 'villages' for workers, with communal spaces enclosed by low-rise and easily accessible buildings. The planning, as well as the architecture, can thus be viewed as a prototype for moderating tropical conditions in order to create a flexible and convivial working environment, to restore connections with nature, and to dramatically reduce energy consumption. The interdependence between the building and the greenery is critical to the significance of this prototype: if the screens of greenery do not work, the building will not work. The symbiosis is primal.

→ pp. 84, 232

Wood in the Sky

Geneva, Switzerland
2009–2012

As in most European cities of a similar size, the central residential districts of Geneva comprise a compact matrix of apartment blocks capped at an identical height. Over the last century, the Geneva building code has generally specified that apartment blocks should have seven floors with a single storey attic. In the face of increasing demand for living space close to the city centre, the regulations were recently changed to allow the addition of another attic level, so that the roofs could now support two floors of apartments.

G8A's seemingly humble extension to the roof-scape of Les Charmilles — one kilometre west of Geneva's railway station — has provided a diversion, a distraction, and a delight to the homogenous scale and repetitive appearance of the precinct. In order to lessen the load, the new structure was built in wood, with a timber cladding that continues over the façade of the existing attic level to eliminate any visual distinction between the new and old layers.

Situated above an orthogonal concrete apartment block, the timber addition can be clearly viewed from the street, and asserts an unexpectedly graceful and lightweight character above the walls of masonry. In order to ensure privacy from other rooftop dwellers, timber frames extend as rectangular extrusions from each apartment, which provides a vision of a crafted autonomous artefact perched above the city.

The three-dimensional compound joinery of Wood in the Sky forms an orthogonal addition to the tiled roof, reinvigorating a cityscape with an urban gesture that was singular and unexpected, yet rational and respectful.

→ pp. 86, 233

Gordon-Bennett

Geneva, Switzerland
2007–2013

The Gordon Bennett project was built according to a prescribed masterplan in the suburbs of western Geneva, and although G8A only designed one of the five low-rise buildings in its entirety, they were — by virtue of designing the extremely conspicuous external balustrades — responsible for the external identity of the development as a whole. Four of the buildings are residential whilst one contains offices, and each of the blocks surrounds a rectangular courtyard.

Unlike the other four blocks, the residents of G8A's building access their apartments from the courtyard, rather than the exterior, after entering through a portal from the wide public walkways of the Gordon Bennett precinct. The landscaped courtyard formed a semi-public space and acts as a transition zone that would be used more frequently than a completely enclosed area, thus encouraging a greater degree of social interaction. The living areas of the apartments open out to this internal courtyard, so that all residents share the views and the use of the gardens.

The entire low-rise development is notable for its sense of communal connectivity, and much of this is derived from the whimsical ornamentation of the black-steel balustrades, which adorn the all-encircling balconies. Although the slender twirling forms of the balustrades were parametrically derived, they look crafted and organic, like the tendrils or long grasses seen in the forms of Art Nouveau. The proliferation of balconies ensures that the private (or semi-private) lives of the occupants are not necessarily internalised, as visual and aural interaction (or sociability) is immediately provided by the proximity of the other apartment blocks. Here is an interstitial balcony-to-balcony relationship, a traditional 'social device' that characterised the densely settled 'old towns' now cherished by proponents of renewed urban densification.

As the balconies cantilever some distance out from the compact blocks, the balustrades define the appearance of the buildings and the project as a whole and provide relief from the rigidity of the pre-determined massing. The device of simple repetition, of duplicating a strong horizontal element — as a vista — throughout a potentially generic development, has been utilised by G8A in several other projects, most conspicuously at Punggol Waterway Terraces in Singapore.

→ pp. 90, 234

Green Ridges

Tampines, Singapore
2013–2018

Erected by the Housing and Development Board and universally referred to as HDBs, Singapore's homogenous public housing blocks have spread relentlessly across the island, swallowing up vast tracts of land whilst simultaneously attempting to display a dedication to the principles of a garden city. This has been quite a balancing act, and to the credit of the Housing Development Board and the Urban Redevelopment Authority, the densely populated city does look green and does function as green (in terms of environmental responsibility). Twenty-three autonomous new towns are surrounded by green belts and large swathes of residual rainforest and are connected with each other by a highly efficient public transport system. As most of the new towns were built before the awareness of the need for sustainable design, their housing blocks did not overtly appear to be green, but many had incorporated methods for passive environmental control: such as north/south orientation in order to avoid direct sunlight, and cantilevered linear balconies that shield the apartments below.

An awakening occurred in the early 21st century, and Singapore gained quite some renown as a pioneer in the field of large-scale green design. Several of the most notable eco-friendly and environmentally aware projects were HDB developments, and G8A's megastructural Punggol Waterway Terraces (2009–2015) was incontrovertibly one of those. In addition to its incorporation of a program for passive energy control (featuring an ingenious strategy for cross-ventilation), the project was distinguished by the luxuriant landscaping of its riverside parkland, encircled by the tapering hexagonal apartment blocks.

Green Ridges, a subsequent HDB development for 2,000 apartments in the new town of Tampines North, did not have the same degree of latitude for typological inventiveness as Punggol (the Housing and Development Board had reverted to a more formulaic construction program promoting a "back to basics" attitude), but the project maintains G8A's passive energy control program and it has a sumptuous public park as its most conspicuous feature. The newly created landscape — known as the Environmental Deck — is elevated on a podium two levels above the street, and it flows around and between four rows of slab blocks. This vast communal garden serves as a pedestrian connection and sequence of relaxation areas, shaded at various times of the day by the apartment blocks and cooled by the breezes funnelled between the buildings and from the car park levels below.

The as-per-regulation site planning was subtly calibrated to relieve the mundane internal vistas of orderly apartments in a row. By staggering the placement of the blocks, shifting them on plan to the north and south, the fixed vanishing points of the typical modernist housing estate have been effectively distorted, and this warping of expectation is exacerbated by the chamfered edges of the floor-slabs, which protrude as brightly painted green strips at every level. The Environmental Deck will form part of continuous parkland wrapping through the northern precinct of Tampines, connected by podium level bridges to other HDB estates currently under construction, in order to create a car-free and people-friendly garden city above the streets

below. Green Ridges should thus not be adjudged as a stand-alone project, but as a component of an organic urban environment, and as it was the first to be completed in north Tampines, it has established a back-to-nature template for the remaining sectors of the precinct.

→ pp. 92, 173, 236

Infinity Village

Hanoi, Vietnam
2017–2121

Infinity Village—the latest stage in the evolution of the Hoa Lac High-Tech Park, to the west of Hanoi—introduces curvilinear forms and a terraced massing to G8A's sequence of horizontal and porous office buildings. High-Tech Landscape, the first completed development at Hoa Lac, instilled principles of interconnectivity and a village-style ambience that did not enclose the space: a three-storey office block with an E-plan and a low-slung rectangular transparent cafeteria set on either side of a public open courtyard. The notion of a self-sufficient communal compound was apparent, but a formal organic entity had not been implemented. An approach of porous enclosure, with a clear sense of potential linkages in a metabolist idiom, was then realised in an adjoining subsequent development named Concrete Lace, a continuous four-storey block on a sharply-angled pentagonal plan centred by a landscaped, semi-public courtyard. The proposition was now clear: the masterplan for Hoa Lac would evolve as a set of porous blocks and enclosed semi-public spaces, with a low-rise horizontality that would harmonise with the existing topography and landscape, and would mimic the courtyard typology of the local villages.

Set opposite those earlier developments on the southern shores of a narrow waterway, the irregular elliptical forms of the Infinity Village step up as a series of grass-roofed layers, from two-storeys at the waterfront to five-storeys at the road entry. The project is significantly larger than the previous developments, but the scale of the massing is alleviated and subverted by the layering and the all-enveloping greenery. As with Concrete Lace, the continuous building block has a rigid width, but here it encloses two courtyards with its sinuous plan. In order to optimise the amount of floor space and to enable workplace flexibility, the structural cores are placed in the courtyards, and their quasi-monumental cylindrical forms appear as a proud manifestation of the metabolic system of structural support. The column-free floor levels are completely glazed, and the views from the courtyard to the buildings and the views to the courtyard from the buildings are more or less inter-changeable: the entire complex has a seamless inside/outside reciprocity that might be described as 'high-tech tropical'.

In a formal sense, the architecture can be appreciated as an appropriate tropical application of the mega-structuralist and metabolist projects devised (and occasionally built) in the late 20th century, but in terms of sustainability and sociability another precedent is equally pertinent. The workplace and community projects designed by the Dutch architects Aldo van Eyck and Herman Hertzberger comprised organic, cell-like collections of spaces, which responded to the needs of workers and residents, and enhanced their social interactions. At Hoa Lac High-Tech Park, and most evidently with the Infinity Village, G8A is patiently constructing a low-rise built environment that encourages a sense of community and wellbeing, and which gently integrates with and respects the natural environment.

→ pp. 99, 153, 238

ICRC
Visitors' Centre

Geneva, Switzerland
2009–2014

Although architecturally unremarkable, the mansion on the hill (built in 1876), which serves as the headquarters for the International Committee of the Red Cross, is an internationally recognised symbol of the Red Cross and the city of Geneva. The accretion of later buildings in the surrounding compound has not been attractive or well planned, but these ancillary structures remain out of sight from the public, who gaze up at the headquarters from the road below. The acclaimed Red Cross Museum (designed by Zoelly, Hafaeli, and Girardet, and opened in 1988) was also hidden from view, as a concrete bunker embedded within the steep slope beneath the headquarter building.

When G8A won the competition to design both a Visitors' Centre and a set of large meeting rooms, they also opted — for two reasons — to minimise any visual impact. Firstly, they wished to retain the stand-alone grandeur of the 19th century building, and secondly, they realised that the agglomeration of other structures on the site was such a mess that potential engagement was impossible. Both of G8A's buildings have a lighter material touch than the Red Cross Museum, and by utilising transparency and reflection, the structures avoid 'confrontation' with any other buildings on the site, whilst providing a much-needed sense of order to the semi-public spaces and circulation routes.

As with the adjacent museum, the two levels of meeting rooms were buried in the steep hillside, only visible to the public as two long thin strips of reflective glass, which provide illumination and views for the occupants. This public presence is architecturally neutral, but it does bestow a topographic sensibility to the site by applying a stepping gradation to the hillside, which slyly accentuates the symbolic value of the mansion on the crest.

The Visitors' Centre, which is primarily a cafeteria, sits on the same hilltop level as the headquarters. With a curvaceous plan, the centre has a totally transparent continuous glass façade topped by a slender flat concrete slab, and this sleek tectonic treatment pays homage to the greater surrounding context of Geneva's international precinct, distinguished by its collection of elegant, post-war, modernist buildings. In combination with the similarly sleek window strips of the meeting rooms, the 'look' of the Visitors' Centre presents a discreet yet significant addition to the international precinct, but G8A's most tangible achievement was the restoration of formal coherence to the unruly agglomeration of buildings on the Red Cross site.

→ pp. 100, 240

Jungle Station

Ho Chi Minh City, Vietnam
2017–2018

The renovation of an architecturally unremarkable printing factory, built in the 1960s near the centre of Ho Chi Minh City, catered in the most architecturally undemonstrative manner to the 'pop-up' inclinations of the contemporary workforce, if not specifically to the millennial generation. The stripped-back casual artlessness of the conversion of a factory into a totally flexible 'co-working' environment could have taken place in anywhere in the world, whether Berlin or Beijing, and is somewhat refreshing to note that such pan-global 'anywhereness' feels right at home in Vietnam, which has no shortage of co-working millenials.

The nonchalance of attitude is made clear before you see the building, because is actually rather difficult to find. The factory is located in a small laneway and is devoid of external enhancement: it is what it was. The elemental post and beam structure, trusses, external walls, and floor slabs of the rectangular two-storey factory were retained, although the upper floor slab and the pitched roof were carved open in a longitudinal slash. This crucial incision brought life and light to a previously dingy and drab interior space, and created a seductive raison d'être for the optimistically entrepreneurial occupants of such a workplace. This central canyon — referred to as the Green Connector — is suffused with daylight

and masses of tropical plants: palm trees reach skyward through skeletal black-painted trusses, whilst vines cascade to the ground floor from herb-filled planter boxes.

The working spaces, arrayed around the central void, have both internal and external views, and their configuration is made endlessly flexible through the use of light weight partitions. Almost hidden within the foliage of the atrium, more casual and socially spontaneous meeting places are set amongst the concrete surfaces of the planter boxes, and interspersed with relaxation areas and a coffee bar. Artworks by Laurent Barnavon hang on the exposed brickwork of the end walls, and their refracted reflective surfaces form a visual extension of the luminous tropical gardens. The absence of any architectonic expression and the unadorned retention of the industrial structure instil a sense of freedom and reinforce the occupants' presumed preference for avoiding professional pressure. By exposing the most basic elements and materials of the existing factory, and by simply inserting the natural delights of sunshine and plant-life, the intervention of G8A is effectively a non-intervention, which is often what the adaptive re-use of a perfectly functional disused building should entail.

→ pp. 107, 242

Nr. 23

La Tuilerie

Geneva, Switzerland
2008–2012

G8A has designed several medium-density housing schemes for the discreetly well-heeled suburbs and villages that line the western shores of Lake Geneva. Most of the citizens would prefer to live in private villas, but land is scarce and townhouse developments must suffice for all but the very rich. The new residents, however, expect some compensation in the form of amenity and environment, and the local community would like to see some tangible benefits.

G8A's scheme for a housing development in the suburban village of Bellevue specifically prioritised the revitalisation of the surrounding neighbourhood, whilst establishing an invigorating natural environment for the new residents. In fact, the landscaping is evidently more important than the buildings, and it demonstrably encloses them, thus inverting the courtyard typology regularly employed by G8A on more constrained sites. La Tuilerie — set well back from the main road and hidden by a row of shops — is comprised of two residential blocks that each contain fifteen apartments. The extroverted nature of the disposition of the architecture, and the newly verdant and spacious landscape have given the village a new focal point and personality.

Previously occupied by a tile factory, the site for the housing was transformed by G8A into a park featuring a revitalised stream, which had been flowing through a covered channel, whilst the basement of the factory was retained and converted into an underground car park. This new landscape, which also features a shallow retaining pond, restored much-needed public space for Bellevue, as the heavy traffic on the main road had inhibited the civic ambience of the village and its lakefront.

Building regulations stipulated the use of a pitched roof, and G8A reduced the external architecture to the point where the flat façades resemble a child's drawing of a house. The two blocks, which each contain fifteen apartments, appear as large and somewhat crudely drawn houses in the parkland. G8A used that simplicity of form and absence of scale as a blank canvas to play abstract games with the window placement and colouring. Square windows and loggias of varying sizes, framed by brightly coloured deep-set reveals, are studded across the grey walls in a pattern that appears to be random, but was in fact determined by sunlight orientation and the local requirement that at least half the wall surfaces must be solid.

→ pp. 110, 244

Nr. 24

Epicentre

Istanbul, Turkey
2011

Topographic architecture has been a continual theme for G8A, and some of their most arrestingly experiential designs have taken advantage of site-specific challenges and opportunities — such as The Birds in Geneva and the Punggol Waterway Terraces in Singapore — or, as in Istanbul, from a client brief that clearly anticipated something theatrical.

Taking inspiration from the otherworldly volcanic landscape of the island of Lanzarote, G8A conceived a dramatic and (literally) fantastic piece of subterranean place-making for a suburban 'no man's land' site near Istanbul Airport. The proposed centre for natural disasters is embedded within a huge 'fissure' cracked open from a folded sloping ground plane, and the immediate impact is poignant, with the phenomenological sensation of an eruption, of an earthquake: an acknowledgment that our natural environment can be dangerous and that our existence is fragile and ephemeral.

Epicentre is entered through three zigzag pathways descending from the street to a public plaza, an open-air void in the centre of the 'fissure', which is overlooked by parkland: a symbol of re-growth on the jagged folds of the new cantilevered ground plane above. The various components of the centre — education facilities, exhibition halls, conference rooms, offices, and a planetarium — are 'buried' beneath the 'earth's crust', so that entire complex has the feeling of a grotto,

of a volcanic cave where we are constantly aware of the capricious nature of our planet's energies.

→ pp. 114, 165, 245

141

Oerlikon

Zurich, Switzerland
2013–2016

An ongoing project in the Neu Erlikon district of northern Zurich is noteworthy for its prioritisation of place-making, rather than architectural statement, and as such represents a European implementation of the experience gained and the strategies applied by G8A in Asia. On a large rectangular site in a windswept area of warehouses and industrial buildings, G8A was commissioned by a private developer to renovate an existing seven-storey tower and provide two new buildings. The entire compound will be occupied by various facilities and departments of ETH University, and presented the opportunity to create a semi-public and semi-autonomous precinct in a neighbourhood devoid of human scale and social interaction.

On the northeast perimeter of the site, the renovated tower block now houses workshops for the architecture department of the university, and a recently completed three-storey block now extends south at a right angle from the tower to the street frontage. This new block, which serves as the post-office for the entire university, will form the eastern edge of a plaza enclosed to the north and west by a new residential building for ETH students. The plaza is elevated above a car park, and when the large residential block is completed, it will be occupied or traversed by a mixture of architecture students, office workers, and student residents, and will accessible to the public from the street on its southern side. An amorphous cloud-like artwork (designed by students of Singapore's SUTD University) will float above the plaza as a giant sunshade.

The three-storey post-office block was placed on the street level, separated from the car park and podium-level plaza by a pocket garden, which enables the afternoon sun to penetrate the lowest level. As the western elevation features two different types of sun shading devices — pivoting mesh screens alternate with a series of retractable white canvas awnings — the appearance of the façade varies according to the weather. The new residential building will be protected from the sun by sliding panels and recessed loggias, in the manner of G8A's earlier Bamboo apartments in Geneva.

The site planning was determined by the integration of the various functions and the interaction between the buildings' occupants, and the purpose of the development was not architectural but rather social. G8A's thought-process might be seen as expedient in a Swiss context, but the architects have become accustomed to an Asian mindset, which views architectural excellence as a bonus rather than a pre-condition. G8A's previous Swiss essays in urban form-making were helped by their congenial locations, but the Neu Erlikon scheme is working on a tabula rasa, and like many new Asian developments, the precinct must create its own social context.

→ pp. 118, 246

Red Houses

Crans-près-Céligny, Switzerland
2006–2008

As with La Tuilerie and Striped Living, the Red Houses residential development aimed to establish a new neighbourhood typology for the semi-rural commuter residential areas that line the lakefront north of Geneva. As Switzerland is rapidly running out of space in which to build and reside, the unfettered construction of individual villas has reached the point where residential areas are encroaching upon arable land and disrupting the delicate existing environmental balance. And, as a corollary, any sense of traditional community and local connectivity is being forsaken in the cause of personal containment.

Although the Red Houses appear as three villas on a flat site, the development actually comprises three, double-storey townhouses, which contain three apartments: one on the ground floor, and two as a duplex on the top floor. A more acceptable degree of densification has been achieved, with a diminished building footprint and the creation of large, semi-public spaces in the form of common gardens. The common gardens are actually fields, rather than plots of manicured flowerbeds, and as the villas possess an unmistakably barn-like appearance, the townhouse development appears typically rural.

At a purely visual level and, it must be observed, at a typological level, the treatment of the site was unequivocally vernacular. With a landscape of simple 'barns' surrounded by fields of long grass, the vista is that of the real countryside, not countrified suburbia. The villas all have large windows, which means that the residents look out to a pastoral panorama rather than personalised (and territorialised) gardens. At a more subtle and sociable level, the village-within-a-village typology reasserts a semblance of traditional community in a rural area, which is being stealthily urbanised without paying heed to local identity and its social morphology. As already noted, the fundamental G8A strategy of instilling a sense of community whilst respecting the environmental context is being implemented at a small-scale in Switzerland, and at the markedly larger and more urban scale of Asia.

The barn-like forms of the Red Houses are abstracted in a deliberately naïve, almost childlike fashion. Coloured reddish-brown, the sheer walls are punctured by rectangular windows and loggias, and surmounted by cleanly-etched pitched roofs, so that the townhouses resemble large rocks or small mountains rising from the grassy meadows. Such an image has become a clichéd Swiss Alpine allusion, but as these representations are so devoid of scale, the townhouses assert a semi-monumental and overtly sculptural presence.

→ pp. 120, 167, 248

Vertical Green City

Hanoi, Vietnam
2016

Away from the historic charms of old Hanoi —the French colonial architecture and the promenades of Hoan Kiem Lake— the city is metamorphosing into a mega-city, and the most conspicuous manifestation of the flight to height is to be found on the western edge of the existing compact city. An elevated highway cuts between rows of recently built towers, none of which are aesthetically remarkable or contextually attuned: they look pretty much the same as most of the high-rise buildings in every Asian city, and they have rigidly adhered to a well-entrenched template for structure and massing.

Hanoi however, has always been a horizontal city, notable for its unimpeded connectivity, and this new verticality (and concomitant segregation) has decisively discontinued those avenues of communication and social interaction. The accepted model for high-rise development in the 'new' Hanoi is a combination of two towers, one commercial and one residential, resulting from a financial equation whereby the sales from the apartments pay for the construction of the office block. The towers are placed on large podiums, the sites are sealed off from the city and from each other, and there is little provision for either public or semi-public space.

G8A's proposal for a typical twin-tower mixed-use project on the eastern side of the elevated highway aimed to reverse the established programmatic template, and to provide a prototype that would reintroduce Hanoi's horizontality to a high-rise precinct. The development was not conceived as two separated towers, but as an interlinked block, which placed the residential and commercial components in the most appropriate locations. The block was vertically segmented, with three volumes stacked above one another and separated by 'plazas in the sky'. To reinstate connectivity and sociability at street level, the entire building was raised above a publicly accessible plaza and gardens. The avowed intention was to create diversity, rather than insularity, and to achieve sustainability whilst retaining sociability.

Apartments occupy two towers in the top segment, separated by and overlooking a 'sky park' for the residents, which spreads across the full breadth of the block. The occupants of the two lower volumes, containing offices and commercial facilities, also have access to a 'plaza in the sky', which slices between the two horizontal blocks. In stark contrast to the visual uniformity of contemporary towers, each of the three volumes has a different façade treatment: the apartments have exposed masonry with individual windows, the central office block is passively shaded by louvres, and the lower commercial segment is glazed, but screened by vertical sun shades.

→ pp. 124, 170, 249

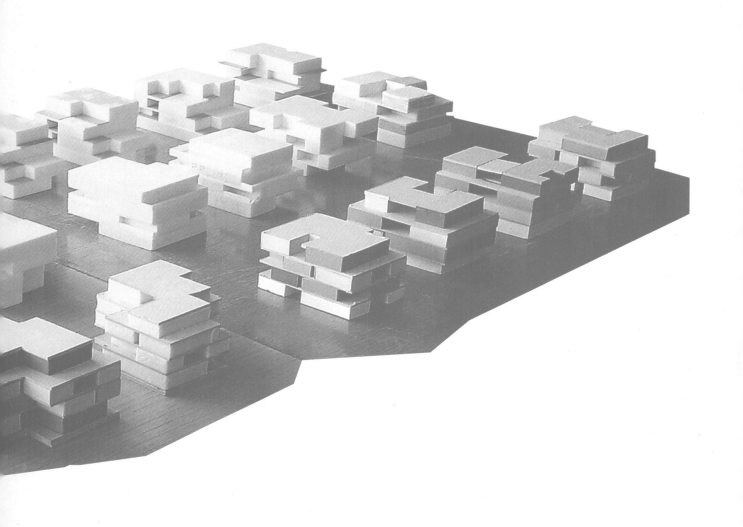

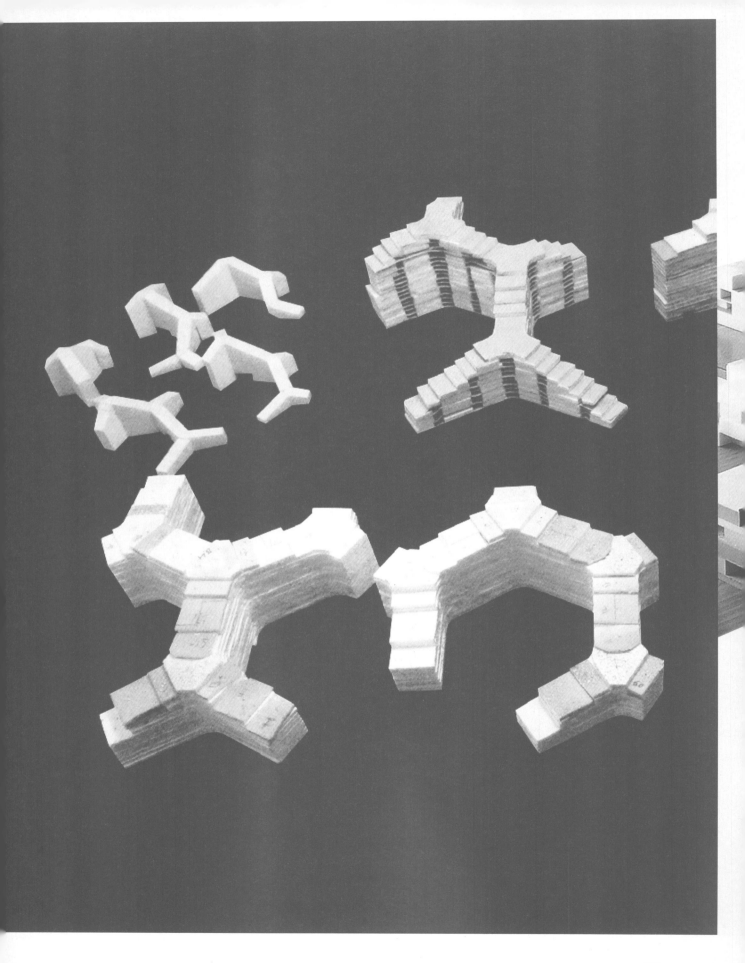

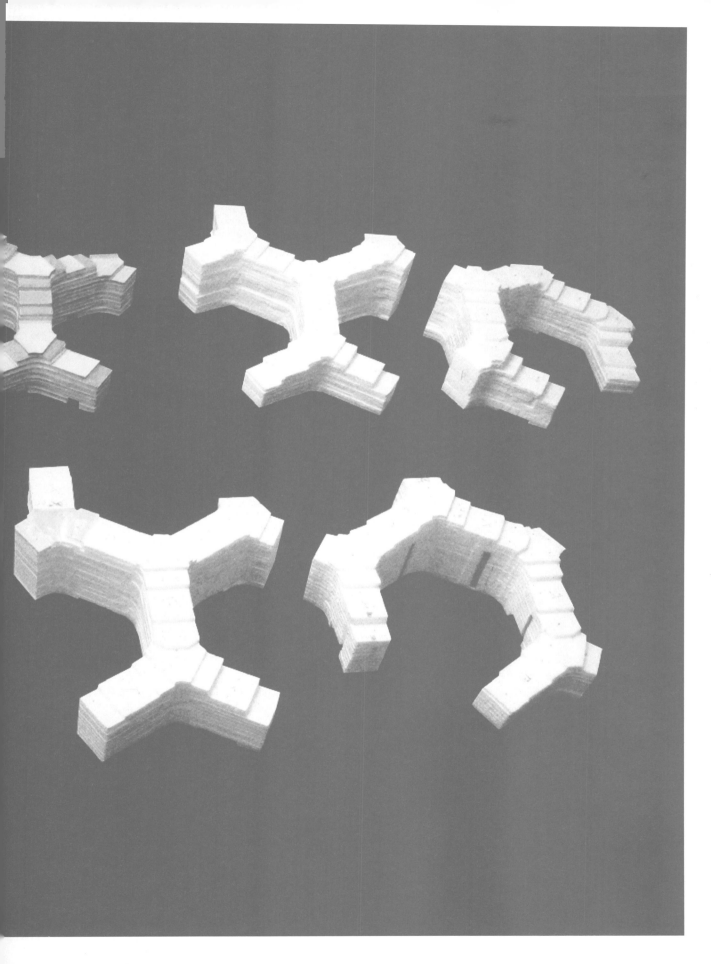

Punggol Waterway Terraces Expressive • Conservative • Duplication • Diversity •
Object • Context • Rationalist • Humanist → **pp. 15, 128, 208**

Trilogy

158

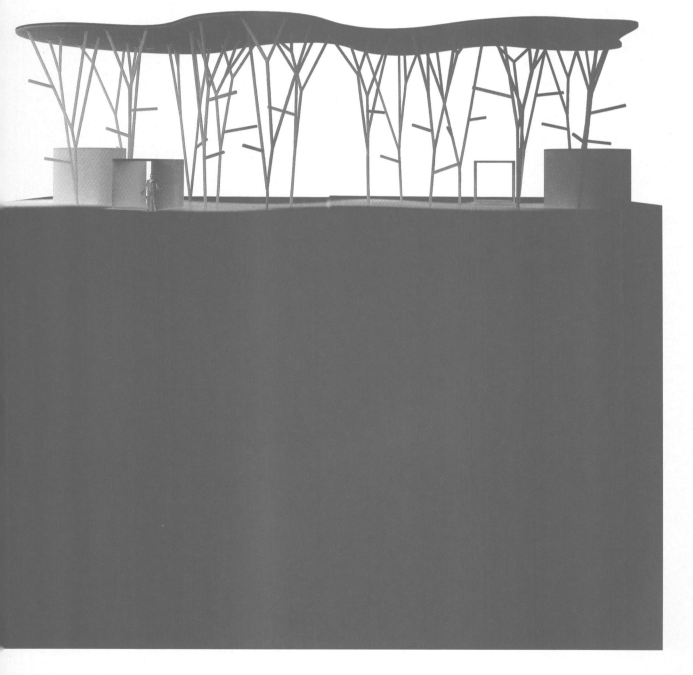

The Birds

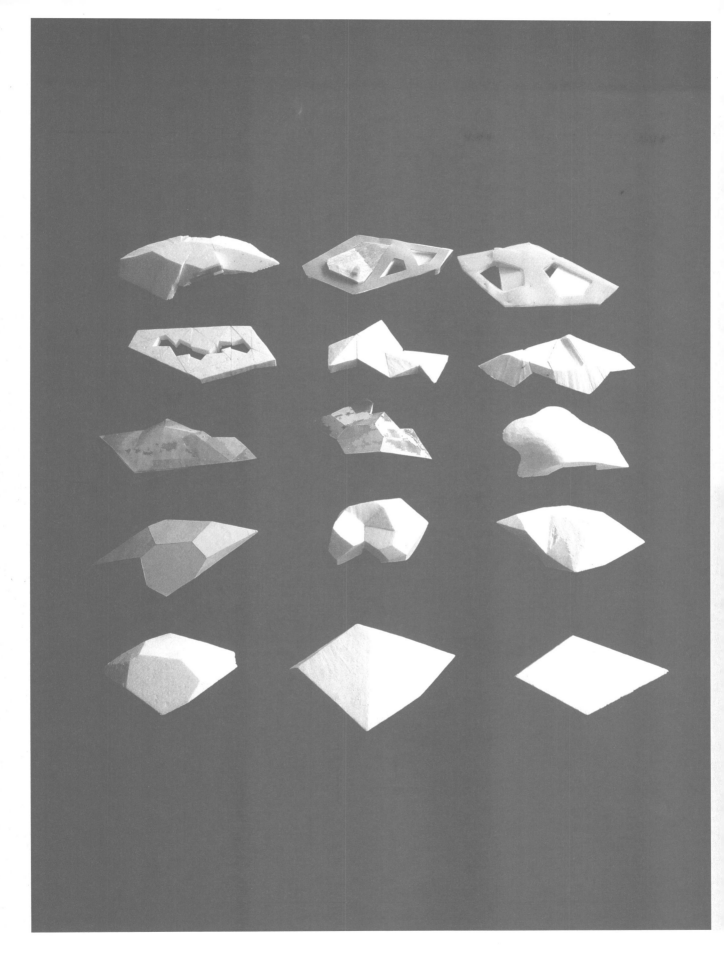

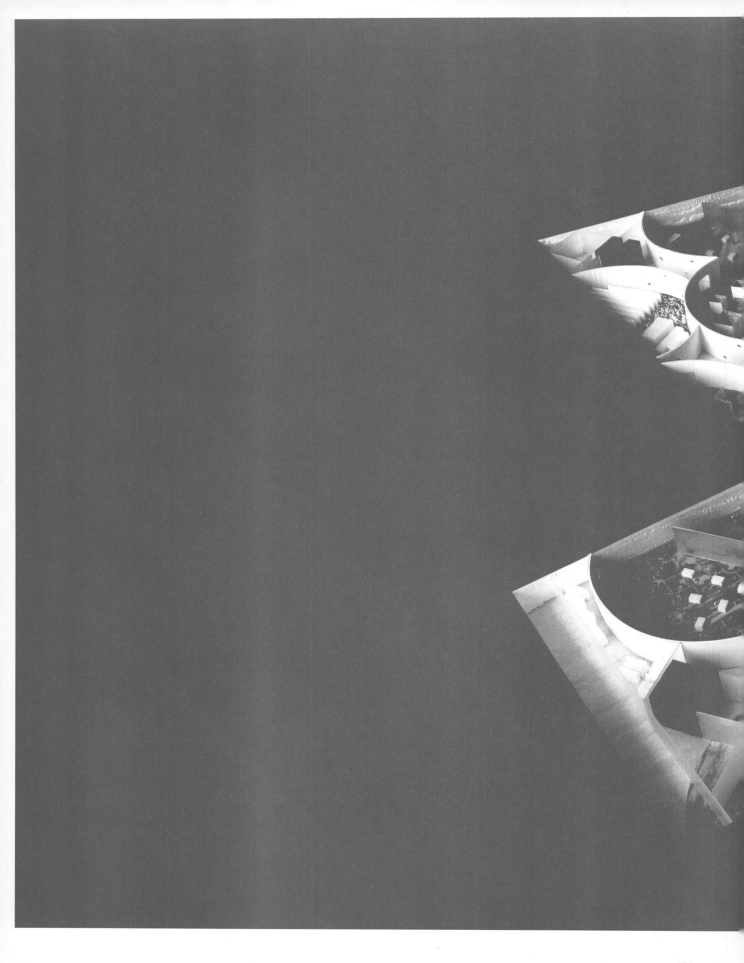

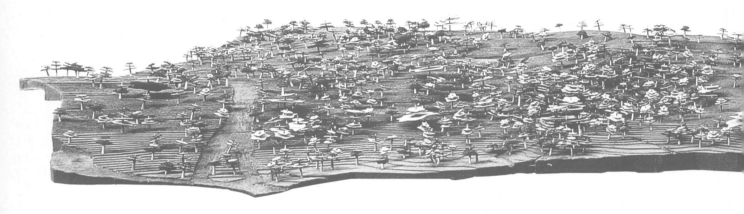

750m

Vista

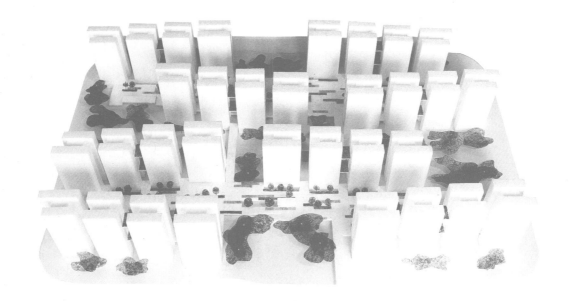

West

East

Many of the apparent contradictions now faced by G8A had been encountered by earlier generations of Western architects who sought work in the developing world, but new and previously unperceived disruptions to programmatic procedure are now unfolding as Asian growth accelerates in the 21st century. Old and new is in itself a perceived contrast between East and West, and an ironic one, as many of the cities and countries we currently refer to as 'new' are steeped in traditions and histories that predate those we refer to as 'old'.

The narrative of 20th century architecture can be reduced to the triumph of modernism and, like it or not, that's how the story continues. Triumph would not be the first word that springs to mind when one surveys a typical modern city, but the ugliness, the inefficiencies, and the societal disruptions that modernism thrust upon us can only be resolved by an evaluation of its history and a discourse upon its future.

In the context of the G8A story, 'modernism' should really be replaced by the term 'International Style', a phrase coined for a 1932 exhibition in New York, which attempted to imbue the nascent modernist buildings of the previous decade with a functional agenda that could underpin the commonalities of the hyper-rational designs. Whilst timely and laudable, this objective was only partially successful (as much of the ensuing architecture was influenced by the look rather than the purpose), yet the use of the word 'international' now appears remarkably prescient. Before World War II, architecture beyond Europe and America was essentially colonial or vernacular, or both. But when the colonial world atomised in the 1940s, the International Style did indeed emerge as an international style: in Latin America, Asia, the Middle East, and Africa. And incontrovertibly, it now had a functional agenda, predicated by its suitability for an equatorial climate and its low-cost construction costs.

The evolution of the International Style, which was an incremental process of expansion from Western Europe, thus provides a neat analogy for the unfolding narrative of G8A. The principal architects of G8A were educated and trained in Western Europe, and began practice in Geneva, where they designed a slew of beautifully detailed and impeccably 'Swiss' buildings. When they secured commissions in Vietnam and Singapore, their as-taught fundamental principles of rational form making and efficient construction were transmogrified for exotic climes, and dramatically rescaled for Asian mega-cities.

It is intriguing to observe that the process is becoming increasingly reciprocal: ideas, methods, and strategies acquired in the East are now being implemented by G8A back in Europe, where many cities are now facing the challenges of increasing population densities and a need for more expedient low-cost construction. And, incidentally, many of the property developers are now Asian.

Both in terms of modes of thinking and methods of construction, many of the contrasts that inform G8A's evolution are actually polarities, so their convergence and resolution is instructive and poignant. Geneva was home to Jean Calvin, the puritanical and parsimonious theologian of the 16th century, and the city and its people have never strayed far from his prescribed constraints. Geneva remains sober, upright, and diligent, and its buildings are notably courteous and compliant. G8A's built projects notwithstanding, Geneva and its architecture are straight-laced, which could never be said about the cities and buildings of Southeast Asia.

A new synthesis of culture…at once European and tropical…and consequently really universalistic in its main designs and techniques.
— Gilberto Freyre

tions that verge on clichés — but even in the rapidly shifting sands of the early 21st century, several critical differences must be acknowledged by an architectural practice. (In the context of this book, East is taken to mean East Asia, and West is taken to mean Europe and the pervading influence of the United States).

The urban scale is markedly dissimilar. The new Asian cities are densely populated, they have been recently and rapidly constructed, the skylines (of the suburbs and new towns as well as the city centres) are increasingly vertical and repetitive, and the street-life is congested and often chaotic.

The climate in tropical Asia could not contrast more emphatically with that of temperate Europe, the quality of construction and materials are generally of a lesser standard in Asia, and (for the most part) the client's budget will also be smaller. The buildings will not be maintained as the architects would desire, and weathering will begin almost immediately. Cold-climate buildings require a compressed plan insulated by solid walls, whilst hot-climate buildings need permeable plans and façades.

Politics and cultures are also distinctively Eastern or Western, although both spheres contain within themselves a multiplicity of contradictions and dissimilarities. Broadly speaking however, an innate sense of respect for family, community, and society is more noticeable in Asian culture, and (possibly not coincidentally) Asian political decision-making tends to flow from the top down, as opposed to the Western democratic ideal of bottom up.

The economies of the Eastern and Western nations are travelling on markedly differing trajectories. The Western economies are pretty much flat-lining, with a less than optimistic outlook, whilst the Eastern economies are (by and large) continuing the surge in wealth creation that accompanied their individual 'emergences' in the late 20th century.

Several critical differences between East and West must be acknowledged by an architectural practice…
— G8A

The slightly dated appellations 'East' and 'West' (or Orient and Occident) do take a set of contrasts for granted — inevitably as generalisa-

Old

New

Old architecture can be a new architecture. When G8A architects speak of 'their ongoing love affair' between West and East, they refer to their adherence to a set of principles that have guided their osmosis between one hemisphere and another.

This continuity of approach serves as a disciplined yet sensitive method to resolve the apparent dilemmas of what might now be considered 'old' and what might now be considered 'new': both in terms of architecture and geopolitical status.

G8A's principles (and the appearance of their buildings) are self-evidently modernist and Western, but that selfsame architectural language has comprehensively defined and defiled the urban landscape of the new Asia, where notions of 'vernacular', 'traditional', and 'regional' have been subsumed by anonymity and uniformity. When first glimpsed in the early flush of regional emergence, the modernist conquest may have been regarded on the one hand as a heroic symbol of liberation, or on the other as a continuation of colonial subjugation, but in the (almost) thoroughly globalised world of the 21st century it must now be viewed with dismay. The architecture of the newly constructed and massively scaled cities is aesthetically banal, and even worse, much of it is contextually and environmentally inappropriate: cold-climate design for hot-climate cities.

In stark contrast — and as a form of reversion to the intentions of their distinguished predecessors in the (pre-air-conditioning) glory days of the International Style — G8A has calibrated their architecture to suit both the context and the climate of the new Asia.

In this age of global warming and urban expansion, what had become old has become new again, and G8A has engaged in extensive research into the prototypes of those predecessors (worldwide, but focused on Southeast Asia) in order to inform their work. The fundamental principles of traditional localised architecture and the International Style are inviolably more sustainable, and more affordable in the long term, than those of the ubiquitous short-term, cost-cutting construction typologies that consume so much energy in the rapidly growing cities. And these fundamental principles are becoming increasingly applicable to austerity struck and rapidly growing cities of the West.

Today I am accused of being a revolutionary. Yet I confess to having had only one master — the past — and only one discipline — the study of the past.
— Le Corbusier

Diversity

Duplication

Diversity

Continuities have distinguished the work of G8A, yet by virtue of the singularly Swiss process of bottom-up deference and consultation, those continuities have been inflected to serve the local context: the climate, the landscape, and the society. In terms of architectural form and structure, the contrasts have cohered, as duplication has embraced diversity. The choice of materials, the façade delineations, topographic awareness, and the landscaping of court yards, are discernible constants in G8A's projects, and they have always been adapted to the context of the site.

The Avenue de France office building (2006–2011) directly overlooks a broad swathe of railway tracks near Geneva's main station with a sheer rectangular elevation comprised of glass panels in a variety of colours. In such a highly visible location, it serves as an urban artwork, and it provides an especially elegant backdrop to the gritty and grimy railways. In chilly Geneva, two layers of glazing are used to capture the morning sunlight, to retain that warmth, and to keep the winds and the noise out. The Coalimex office building (2008–2013), located in a medium-rise commercial precinct of Hanoi, is also sheathed by a sheer double-layered glass façade, which would be instantly recognised as a 'stable-mate' of the Avenue de France building (if anybody were ever to visit both neighbourhoods). As the Coalimex building faces north, it is not penetrated by direct sunlight, so the façade was specifically designed to reduce the noise from a typically hyperactive Hanoi street. The external layer of glass was printed with an opaque abstracted pattern to — once again — provide an urban artwork (or, as G8A would have it, 'an urban fresco').

G8A's obsessive interest in materials has defined the appearance of its architecture. A consistently identifiable house style has been created by the external patterns, rhythms, and interplay of materials, which have evolved from project to project. Façade crafting has been ever-present, and variations and modifications to the core G8A themes have produced a diversity of 'urban frescos'. An analogy with musical composition is quite apposite: as composers, G8A might write songs (or symphonies) that could be performed by different musicians with different instruments; as architects, they 'compose' structures that can be built by different contractors with different materials in different locations.

The details are not the details. They make the design.
— Charles Eames

Duplication

G8A's earlier built projects are notable for the precision of their façade detailing. Two Geneva buildings — the Coral apartments (2007–2011) and the Avenue de France offices (2006–2011) — are essays in fastidious glazing, as is their initial Hanoi project, the Coalimex building (2008–2013). Coral and the adjoining Bamboo (2007–2011) also feature brightly coloured sun-shading devices: multi-hued vertically adjustable screens of fabric adorn Coral, whilst Bamboo has horizontally sliding panels of green glass.

In a village to the north of Geneva, the Striped Living townhouses (2007–2012) are clad in screens of chiselled travertine battens, which are punctuated by recessed window bays. The nearby La Tuilerie apartments (2006–2012) are also studded by an array of recessed windows with colourful reveals, as are the walls overlooking the garden courtyards of the Gordon Bennett apartments (2007–2013) in western Geneva. The Gordon Bennett apartments, grouped around a set of landscaped plazas and walkways, have a lively disposition: painted apple green, and encased on every floor by cantilevered balconies with organically etched metal balustrades. Ornamental organic patterns are likewise incised from the black external steel framework of the Coral apartments. The emphatic and decorative horizontal expression of such projects as Coral, Bamboo, and Gordon Bennett, was extended at a larger scale when G8A secured comissions in Asia. The Punggol Waterway Terraces (2009–2015) were built in white-painted concrete, and the enormous massing of the two housing blocks was ameliorated by a seemingly infinite series of horizontal striated bands, which serve as both sunshades and balconies on every level. Upon closer inspection, it can be seen that these undulating strips were once again embellished by organic ornamentation in the form of leaf-shaped cut outs. As glimpsed behind the waves of white concrete, the walls of the apartments were painted in four different hues of green in order to create a subliminal sense of localised identity in such a large complex. The protruding floor-slabs and the roof of the Concrete Lace office building (2014–2017), on the outskirts of Hanoi, were forcefully expressed on the elevations, and this horizontal framework was dynamically intersected by sets of zigzagging columns. The floor slabs and columns serve as sun shading devices, which will also support greenery.

Concrete Lace comprises the third stage of G8A's masterplan for the Hao Lac High-Tech Park on swampy flatlands west of Hanoi, and the two previous buildings represented an adaptation of earlier schemes. The long southern lakeside elevation of the High-Tech Landscape building (2011–2013) bears more than a passing similarity to the Bamboo apartments, but in such a sun-struck setting, the green glass panels are co-opted in the name of passive energy control. The other elevations are screened by swivelling vertical strips of timber (featuring rice-grain shaped perforations) and by layers of vegetation. An adjoining pavilion called The Dots (2013–2014), comprising a single level open-plan cafeteria and relaxation area, formed a tropical adaptation of the restaurant at the Red Cross Visitor's Centre (2009–2013) in Geneva. A thin concrete roof floats above the glass-walled cafeteria, and the space is 'tropicalised' by glazed circular courtyards filled with lush stands of bamboo. As with the Red Cross restaurant and The Birds (2007–2008) — a steel-mesh aviary in Geneva — the façade is a non-façade, it is invisible, which means that the identifiably G8A formal expression results from the clearly visible articulation of the internal structure.

Quite deliberately, many of G8A's façades can now be read as a depiction of the internal structure, no matter whether the external elevations are transparent, semi-transparent, or clad with timber and masonry: the body of the building is not disguised or camouflaged by the clothes it wears. As G8A states… "You will always see the skeleton of the building."

Intriguingly, one of G8A's earliest significant Geneva proposals was for an office building clad by screens of deciduous vines, which would shield the workers from summer heat

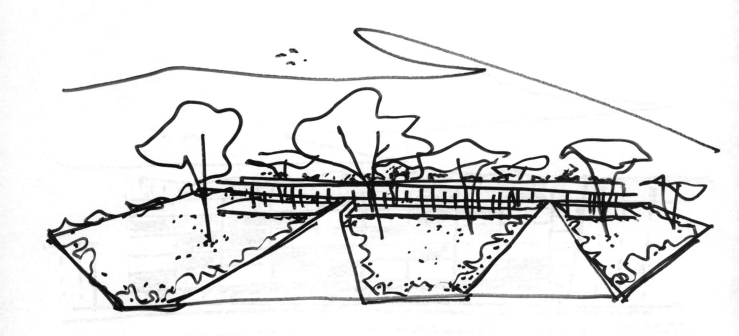

and allow sunlight penetration in winter. Called the Green House, the scheme won a 2003 competition for sustainable architecture (held by Geneva's Department of Territory), and although the offices were never built, the renderings show a building that looks tropical. Curiously prophetic (as G8A had no plans to head East at that time), the project was a precursor for many of G8A's Asian buildings, and indeed for the vine-clad 'walls of green' that now proliferate in tropical cities.

Cold-Climate

Hot-Climate

Cold-Climate

The heat of tropical Asia can be seriously debilitating and, thanks to global warming, the climate is getting hotter. Mechanical ventilation and cooling have provided a most efficacious relief, but that solution has now become a major problem. Living and working without air-conditioning has become almost unthinkable, but we are paying a high price: both in terms of its operational costs and its contribution to global warming. The cold-climate model of construction — floor slabs cantilevered from a central core and enclosed by a curtain wall — has been implemented throughout the cities of tropical Asia, for housing and commercial use, but its blatant unsuitability — no ventilation or sun-shading — can only be mitigated by air-conditioning and heat-resistant glazing. Given the requirements and strictures of commercial activity, it is difficult to see how a formula can be devised for a completely sustainable office tower (i.e. one that is solely reliant upon passive energy sources) without drastically rethinking the nature of workplaces themselves, and by persuading property developers to reassess their bottom-line financial equations. Housing, however, is a different story.

Apartment (or public housing) blocks were built in the tropics before the widespread use of air-conditioning, and the methods for ventilation and cooling were fundamentally those that had always been used. Essentially, the apartments required cross-ventilation, they were shaded by overhangs and sunscreens, and were orientated to avoid the heat of the afternoon sun in particular. Many of the architects — especially in Latin America — took advantage of these prerequisites to concoct designs that were wonderfully expressive, such as Oscar Niemeyer's Edificio Copan (1952–1966) and Edificio Niemeyer (1954–1960), both of which had a sinuous plan and were completely wrapped by continuous bands of slender sensuous brises-soleils. Both in terms of architecture and urban planning, possibly the

most influential large-scale housing projects in Southeast Asia (and possibly Asia as a whole) were constructed in Singapore after the country became independent in 1965, and the initial developments comprised rows of concrete slab-blocks constructed as a tropical-necessity modernist-design hybrid. Their north-south façade orientation minimised sun penetration, and single-loaded open-air communal corridors both stimulated cross-ventilation and shaded the units below. As Singapore grew more affluent and as global architectural fashions changed, those semi-heroic tropical-modernist forms quietly disappeared, to be replaced by blocks whose designs were increasingly generic (many were assertively 'post' modern) and whose construction was unsustainably non-tropical. The apartment plans were hermetic rather than permeable: they were artificially cooled and sealed in. And, not coincidentally, the developments became increasingly anti-social.

Before air-conditioning, mental concentration and with it the quality of work deteriorated as the day got hotter and more humid. Historically, advanced civilisations have flourished in the cooler climates. Now, lifestyles have become comparable to those in temperate zones, and civilisation in the tropical zones need no longer lag behind.
— Lee Kuan Yew

Hot-Climate

Air-conditioning is commonly cited as the main reason for Singapore's remarkable economic success story, but by the beginning of the 21st century, its residents had become so accustomed to the ubiquity and efficiency of 'aircon' that they had lost touch with natural methods of cooling. It became evident to town-planners, and to some enlightened architects, that — both on the grounds of energy usage and social cohesion — the trend should be redressed in the public housing estates, which house eighty-two percent of Singapore's population. Air-conditioning accounted for a third of each household's energy consumption, its

adverse effect on climate change was now acknowledged, and Singapore's sense of community had been steadily eroded to the point where it was described as 'the air-conditioned nation', a country whose residents had retreated from their convivial tropical habitat to artificially chilled comfort zones. At the very least, a trade-off could be encouraged, whereby natural methods of ventilation and shading could be augmented by the occasional use of air-conditioning, whilst a communal lifestyle could be restored by the re-introduction of open-air public corridors and decks, and by apartment plans that facilitate a connection with the outside world.

In Singapore, in the field of public housing, the pendulum is now swinging back to the principles and the forms of tropical-modernist design.

G8A won the 2009 competition for the Punggol Waterway Terraces public housing with a scheme that deliberately sought to 'commemorate' the spirit and ideals of Singapore at the time of its independence in 1965, and the architects actually asked…"Is Singapore still brave enough for Utopia?" After so many decades of urban desecration wrought by the cynical commodification of modernist ideals, the notion of Utopia in architecture had been ignominiously discarded, and G8A was being quite brave in retrieving it from the garbage. But the modernist vision of Utopia — particularly as built at the zenith of the International Style — had already proven to be adaptable and fundamentally appropriate to tropical living (but not for housing estates in cities such as St Louis and Glasgow, where the utopian towers have been demolished in the cause of civic pride and human dignity).

The Punggol Waterway Terraces utilised a matrix of planning strategies to provide passive climatic control, whilst maximising the orientation of the apartments towards the waterway that bisects the site. Situated on linked hexagonal plans, the 'arms' of the blocks step down to the waterway as terraces, so all the residents have a direct experiential connection with the landscape and with their community. The apartments are shielded from the heat and the rain by undulating ribbons of 'Juliet' balconies, which perform as decorative sun-shading devices.

By virtue of an ingenious planning manoeuvre on the part of G8A, the double-loaded corridors (which usually impede airflow to the apartments) actually facilitate cross-ventilation and vertical cooling. Due to the geometry of the hexagonal block plans, three corridors are angled at 120 degrees from the lift cores to serve apartments grouped in threes. Each apartment is directly ventilated by the lift-core breezeways and by voids inserted between the groupings, and every room is open to fresh air. Traditional principles of passive tropical design have thus been inventively recalibrated and then expressed at a monumental scale. In addition, the contextually-attuned planning and massing have reintroduced a sense of neighbourhood, and the breezy light-filled corridors (which extend for over half a kilometre on each floor) encourage spontaneous social interaction.

Expressive

Conservative

A new highway extends due west for thirty kilometres from Hanoi across cleared flatlands, before stopping abruptly near the foothills of the mountain ranges that encircle the city. In the manner of so many cities of 'emerging' Asia, these flatlands are waiting for the as-decreed urban expansion, which will turn Hanoi into a new Shenzhen, which was a new Shanghai, which was a new Hong Kong. But for the moment, the three-lane highway — with an ornate series of streetlights and exit ramps — is conspicuously under utilised. One presumes that will not last.

At the end of the road, the Hoa Lac High-Tech Park is slowly taking shape. The renderings on the billboards show a brave new cityscape of gleaming towers, tree-lined boulevards, and rings of factories, but the landscape is currently a dusty terrain of occasional building sites surrounded by muddy lagoons. Several small clusters of buildings have already risen from the sunburnt plains, and the workers are bussed in and out daily. In 2011, G8A drew up the masterplan for Hoa Lac, and they have designed the initial buildings: a low-rise office complex and a multi-function pavilion on a waterfront site, which have now been adjoined by a four-storey office block called Concrete Lace. When viewed (and photographed) during construction in early 2016, the structure of Concrete Lace was at its most skeletal, a bony assemblage in raw concrete with extruded floor slabs and cranked columns of equal width. Evocatively coloured by the late afternoon sun, the structure appeared as a 'romantic ruin', a heroic vision in a most unlikely setting.

Heroic visions were central to the success and failure of modernist architecture, and the International Style in particular. Now justly repositioned in the canon of architectural significance, the flamboyant expressionism of the International Style in the hands of such architects as Oscar Niemeyer drew quite some opprobrium at the time, although the

ever-sagacious Mies van der Rohe had already articulated a responsible resolution (cohesion) between expression and purpose in 1940 when he explained his design for the Illinois Institute of Technology... "It is radical and conservative at once." This Miesian dictum, that structural expression should be underpinned by rational sobriety, has held sway since the 1950s, much to the despair of those who delight in tectonically driven architecture (and it has to be observed, however ruefully, that the capricious forms made possible by digital technology cannot be classified as structural expression, but as contorted abstraction).

"The external structure is permanent. You will always see the skeleton of the building. This is the 'sustainable ruin'."
— G8A

The appearance of Concrete Lace is pitched somewhere between the classical rigour of Mies and the tectonic indulgence of Niemeyer, as are many of G8A's other Asian projects. A reversion to organic (tropical) expression is tempered by a conservative appraisal of the building's context and function. The structural expression of Concrete Lace and The Dots (2013–2014) in Hanoi, of Punggol Waterway Terraces (2009–2015) in Singapore, and of the Jakob Factory (2015–) in Ho Chi Minh City was determined by the renewed requirements for passive sun-shading and ventilation, and by a desire to respond to the context of the site.

After many years of practice in Asia, G8A has now formulated a rationale for a building's structure and expression. Concrete Lace did resemble a 'romantic ruin' in that fleeting moment when the structure was complete, but the external cladding had not been applied. Rather more pragmatically, however, G8A explains that Concrete Lace was designed with the avowed intention of constructing a sustainable ruin'. G8A's singularly Swiss training prioritised structure above all else, and it was considered mandatory that all architecture must be underpinned by an understanding of

engineering. In a cold-climate environment, the structure is comprised of brick or concrete walls, with 'envelopes' of insulation that serve as a thermal bridge to protect the interior from the cold and damp weather. In tropical Asia, however, the floor slabs can extend beyond the envelope, and the walls become secondary to the structure. As the external cladding plays a diminished (or transitory) role, the columns and floor slabs can thus be read on the façade as 'the external expression of the structure'.

Concrete Lace represents G8A's first resolved application of the 'sustainable ruin'. The columns were placed outside the plan, in order to provide greater internal space and flexibility and to serve as elemental sun shading devices, like great chunks of rock or tree trunks. As it was presumed that the skin of the building would be glass, and would be subject to budgetary restrictions, G8A only conceived of the building in its skeletal form. External cladding, landscaping, and internal partitions, usually have a short lifespan in a tropical environment: any such accretions would be temporary whilst the structure remained permanent.

Much like a ruin, the image of Concrete Lace will always be the external structure, but crucially, this 'ruin' will be sustainable: it provides a flexible framework for any future inhabitation. This strategy represents a breakthrough for G8A, and potentially for all large-scale Asian building development, which has generally treated structure as little more than a method to hold a building together. Both for economic and sustainable reasons, G8A has proposed (and built) a robust structure that, by virtue of its plan, provides additional and highly flexible floor space. In the face of reality, G8A has relinquished their Swiss obsession with detailing, and with their notion of the 'sustainable ruin' they have acknowledged a new contemporary value for architecture. As Mies van der Rohe suggested, this could be both radical and conservative... "It is radical in accepting the scientific and technological driving and sustaining forces of our time. It is conservative as it is not only concerned with a purpose but also with a meaning, as it is not only concerned with a function but also with an expression."

Object

Context

Object

Switzerland is dominated and defined by its landscape. And, possibly more than any other nation, it is renowned for the beauty of its landscape. Switzerland's cities and buildings cannot compete with their settings, they can only complement, which has led to a pervading attitude of deference from its architects. The two best-known Swiss architectural practices — Herzog & de Meuron and Peter Zumthor — are Pritzker Prize winning architectural A-listers who represent the two sides of the Swiss coin. Peter Zumthor has an almost mythological reputation as the alpine craftsman, with his collection of exquisitely detailed and poetic ruminations on phenomenological experience. Herzog & de Meuron, on the other hand, are quintessentially urban architects, with a catalogue of works that respond to a wide variety of urban contexts. An overriding awareness of 'place' — whether rural or urban — has determined and defined the work of both practices.

Switzerland possesses the ultimate in bottom-up governance, with a constitution that devolves the processes of power as they rise from the common people to the regional cantons to the federal government. Communal approval (or disapproval) dictates what can be done and what can be built, and anybody can object, which for an architect presents a unique creative conundrum, most successfully resolved by consultation, by a degree of humility, and by the afore-mentioned deference. The Swiss architect abroad is thus innately attuned to work with, rather than against, the local context, and the notion of 'iconic' architecture is something of an alien concept. G8A describes its approach to devising a distinctive piece of architecture as…"Creating an identity through engaging with the context and culture, and responding to a variety of manmade and natural conditions."

Many of G8A's buildings have engaged with their locations in the most deferential way possibly: they have simply disappeared. The Avenue de France office building (2006–2011) in Geneva is clad entirely with glass panels, so that the façades serve as a modulated and subtly hued mirror of the city and the sky. The only visible components of the Birds aviary (2007–2008), which serves as an unobtrusive 'gateway' to a Geneva park, are slender arboreal columns and an elliptical roof canopy. The two levels of conference rooms in the Red Cross Visitors' Centre (2009–2013) are inserted within a sloping bank beneath the neoclassically stolid Red Cross headquarters, and when viewed from the street below they appear as glazed horizontal slits in a grass-covered bunker. This building-as-a-bunker theme was continued with the Epicentre competition entry (2011) for Istanbul, which located a disaster prevention and education centre in 'fissures' carved beneath the ground plane, and with the Hanoi Parliament Museum scheme (2014), which was placed within a curved 'hillock' in the forecourt of the new Parliament complex.

The concept of 'buildings as landscape' or 'architecture as topography' has resolved the contradictions of the Swiss bottom-up desire to please, and the Asian top-down desire to impose. The Punggol Waterway Terraces is a massive structure, but it was visualised as a piece of topography, as a series of hillsides with terraces that stepped down to the landscape, alluding to the rice-growing paddy fields of Southeast Asia. The Green Ridges public housing project (2013–) in Tampines, Singapore, was conceived as a landscape rather than a building development, where rows of apartments — with varying heights on a staggered site plan — shade the 'green canyons' of public parkland.

"We are typically Swiss…before thinking of the architectural appearance, we must decide the contextual benefit."
— G8A

Context

G8A has increasingly utilised the juxtaposition of mass and void (object and landscape) in the masterplanning of their sites. Concrete Lace (2014–2017) on the outskirts of Hanoi comprises an office building with a permeable pentagonal donut plan enclosing a large communal courtyard, whilst the Jakob Factory (2015–) in Ho Chi Minh City conjoins hollowed rectangular plans to form a permeable matrix, which will contain three courtyards. The masterplan of Punggol Waterway Terraces (2009–2015) provides a form of semi-enclosure, which allows the landscaped hexagonal courtyards to open out and tumble down to the riverbanks.

The scale of Punggol Waterway Terraces is such that the plan is not only relevant to the site itself: as G8A observed in their research of Hong Kong housing typologies… "The act of building was not only about the architecture and its site, it now formed a correlation between architecture and urbanism." The Punggol project is not a discrete or insular set of apartments: it is unequivocally just another part of the densely populated new towns, within which over eighty percent of Singaporeans live. As much as creating architecture, G8A is creating urban form, and all that entails.

Urban form is the stage-set for community life in our increasingly urban world, and three fundamental social zones need to be provided and maintained: public, semi-public, and private. Cities that have grown up over centuries, if not millennia, are engrained with public plazas and markets, semi-public courtyards and cafés, and private apartments or townhouses (which actually retain a degree of community awareness). But can new towns, built with a modernist template on a blank slate, ever successfully replicate the social urbanity of the long-established cities and neighbourhoods of Asia and Europe? When seen in terms of community, the Ville Radieuse model of Le Corbusier (built in blind faith at a massive scale over the last few decades) has been an ignominious failure. Taking heed of that modernist failure, the creation of urban form must now learn lessons from the (pre-modernist) past, and if anything, it should overcompensate residents and workers for the feature-free tabula rasa environment that surrounds them.

G8A's masterplan for the Hoa Lac High-Tech Park, west of Hanoi, was specifically inspired by the small villages of the region, which were arranged around communal courtyards. The Hoa Lac development comprises a series of low-rise buildings centred by semi-public courtyards and surrounded by public parks and gardens. The entire complex, currently under construction, meanders — with little hint of a grid — along the banks of existing lakes and rivers, and will eventually link up with the neighbouring villages themselves. Three buildings are already occupied, and their

sites appear to be seamlessly conjoined as the workers stream across a village-like landscape. The architecture is recessive, not assertive, and an interactive communal environment has been established by reinterpreting the traditional local typology with an adaptable organic module: cellular, molecular, and metabolist. Even though the size of the High-Tech Park will be very large, the urban form will have a diminutive and humanising scale.

Humanist

Rationalist

Humanist

The principles of ensuring that the landscape and the context matter just as much (if not more) than the building, and that open spaces must occupy sizable chunks of a permeable masterplanning matrix, are intrinsic to both sustainable architecture and sociable architecture. In the overheated cities of Asia, where nary a park nor forest can be found, the reintegration of the city with the natural environment is desperately needed. And in both Asia and Europe, the rethinking of a new building's relationship with its urban context, treating it with respect rather than disdain, signals a welcome return to social cohesion and civic pride.

The architecture of G8A is modernist and it is rational, but those ubiquitous attributes are intertwined with an understanding of and a desire for community life. It is a humanist architecture. Possibly to a greater extent than in any other European nation, social responsibility and community spirit have been intrinsic to the stability of Switzerland, and all G8A's Swiss projects (large and small) are notable for the lack of demarcation between public and private spaces, and for their integration within their neighbourhoods. Four housing projects designed in 2006 and 2007 — Striped Living, Coral and Bamboo, La Tuilerie, and Gordon Bennett — operate seamlessly as part of the public realm: they do not impose or retreat, but extend and facilitate, and it is difficult to delineate their site boundaries. Their landscaping and courtyards assimilate with adjoining public and private spaces, and the outlook from each apartment is friendly and neighbourly. Inclusiveness is favoured over isolation, and desirable densification has been achieved without desecrating the landscape.

The more recently designed Neu Erlikon (2012–) project, for the ETH University in northern Zurich, is more assertive in its desire to create community, undoubtedly due to its location in a currently unsociable industrial area, but it also reflects G8A's experience of working for many years in Asia. The development is not notable so much for its architecture than for its ambition to establish an interactive sociable community in a mixed-use urban precinct. An open-air podium, raised above the car park and open to the street on one side, serves as a semi-public courtyard surrounded by two administrative buildings and a residential block now under construction. The intention and the plan are similar to many of G8A's projects in Vietnam, most notably the small-scaled precincts of the Hoa Lac High-Tech Park, which also needed to create socially stimulating environments where none had previously existed. G8A states that it thinks in terms of "…organically linked structures and courtyards, rather than isolated objects surrounded by leftover spaces."

G8A has recognised the benefits of applying Asian solutions for urban density and social cohesion to the rapidly growing districts of European cities, suggesting that a pragmatic Asian approach to the economy and speed of construction could resolve many of the challenges now faced in the West. In terms of recent history this would, of course, represent a 'reverse process': from East to West rather than West to East.

Both Zurich and Geneva are now experiencing a housing shortage, but the building development and construction process in Switzerland can take up to twenty years, whereas G8A notes that "…in Singapore it only takes four." The Swiss architect is famously preoccupied by detail, but such fastidiousness now appears counterproductive in humanist terms, as the design process is (possibly innately) more concerned by the creation of an artefact than by the provision of accommodation. As G8A has now become so accustomed to the Asian approach to construction at a large scale, they are now advocating a rational cohesion of Swiss rigour with Asian speed and flexibility, but a prevailing mindset (mainly bureaucratic) needs to be overcome.

Rationalist

The need for sustainable design and construction is now universally acknowledged, even if it is generally implemented (or partially implemented) in a gratuitous and expedient fashion. The requirement for sociable architecture, however, has had a less tangible advocacy, but it must be recognised that sustainability and sociability go hand in hand: one cannot proceed without the other. The desire to overcome global warming is, after all, a purely social concern: we want the human race to survive.

The greatest legacy of modernist architecture and planning is the 21st century city. Nearly every office tower is sheathed in a curtain wall (as per Mies van der Rohe), nearly every housing estate is comprised of regimented rows of linear blocks (as per Le Corbusier), and most of the other buildings are a combination of the two. The original principles were idealistic — heroic and utopian — but they were not humanist, they were just plain rational. Logic prevailed over life. In Hanoi, however, life has always prevailed over logic. Until recently.

The Old Quarter of Hanoi is about as lively as a city precinct can get: every street is named after the products it sold or the craft it produced, and in terms of street life, nothing much has changed since the 15th century. It is crowded, noisy, colourful, and cheerful, and its building typology is resolutely horizontal and accessible. But beyond the Old Quarter and the area surrounding Hoan Kiem Lake, Hanoi is 'modernising' with unseemly haste, and inevitably, the design and construction template is vertical and inaccessible. The contrast between the conviviality of the Old Quarter and the soullessness of the new housing estates and commercial precincts is incongruous, to say the least.

The elemental benefits of modern architecture cannot be denied by anybody, but such a conspicuous relinquishment of social interaction should not be part of the deal.

As noted by Hasan Uddin-Khan, the "idea of social responsibility…found a resonance in the liberation struggles in Latin America, Asia, and Africa [and] modern architecture was… a symbolic manifestation of a new political and social reality." The 20th century liberation struggles of Asia did not occur simultaneously, some were bloodier than others, and the subsequent relevance of architecture as a symbolic manifestation of social cohesion has fluctuated considerably. As already observed, the Punggol Waterway Terraces by G8A consciously sets out to 'commemorate' the spirit and ideals of Singapore at the time of its independence. But G8A's real intention was to restore — rather than commemorate — those ideals, because socially responsible architecture in an increasingly affluent country had disappeared from the radar. The Waterway Terraces can be viewed as a greatly up-scaled version of G8A's housing projects in Geneva, and the complex was so large that any assimilation with adjoining neighbourhoods was as much an internal exercise as external. G8A's ongoing research into theoretical and as-built global prototypes for mass housing was just as motivated by their sense of 'social responsibility' as it was by the need for sustainable design. The indisputably humanist (verging upon socialist) schemes of Aldo Van Eyck, Moshe Safdie, Paul Rudolph, and Affonso Eduardo Reidy serve as clear precedents for G8A proposals, which address the needs and the identity of the community as well as the corporation.

Exactly what can be achieved in Vietnam is not yet clear. The country endured the most debilitating of all the liberation struggles, and no form of architectural manifestation of its new reality has yet emerged, either in terms of social responsibility or national identity. Appropriately enough, it would appear that Vietnam has not hastened to commission architectural monuments to its new identity, but as with all other countries in 'emerging' Asia, it is to be hoped that social responsibility — rather than expedient development — is prioritised. Rational construction and humanist ideals can be synchronised, and presumed contrasts can converge and cohere.

The idea of social responsibility, engendered by socialism and industrialisation, found a resonance in the liberation struggles in Latin America, Asia, and Africa. Hence it was not surprising that modern architecture was to them …a symbolic manifestation of a new political and social reality.
— Hasan-Uddin Khan

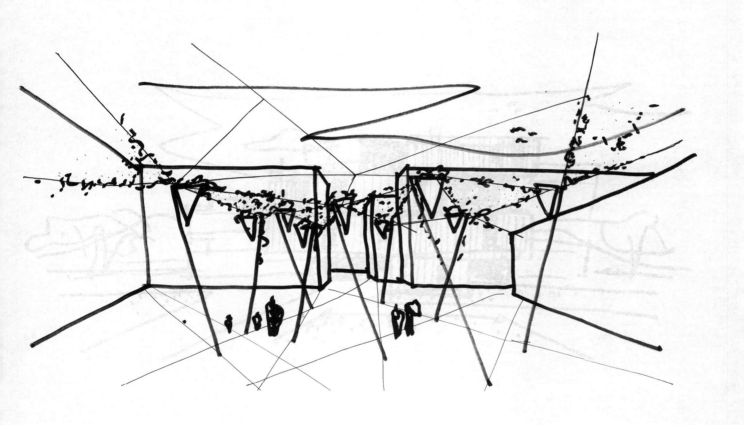

Narratives, models, pictures and drawings are used equally in G8A's practice as displayed here in segregated chapters. Plans, sections and elevations are treated in parallel in the following chapter. Projects are classified by size, then represented by a designated colour expressing the spatial identity of each. The concave or convex colour surfaces highlight the search for a "mass" and "void" balance entering the exploration of concepts of interior and exterior, representing relationships between greyscale and colour, volume and surface.

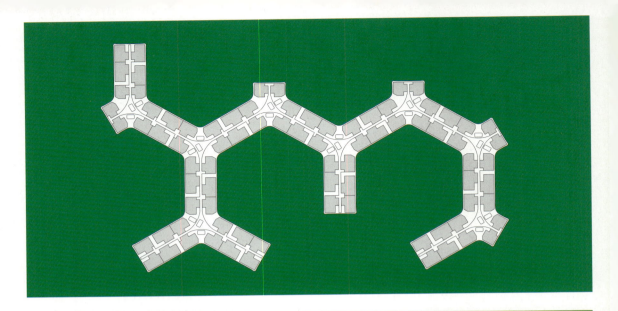

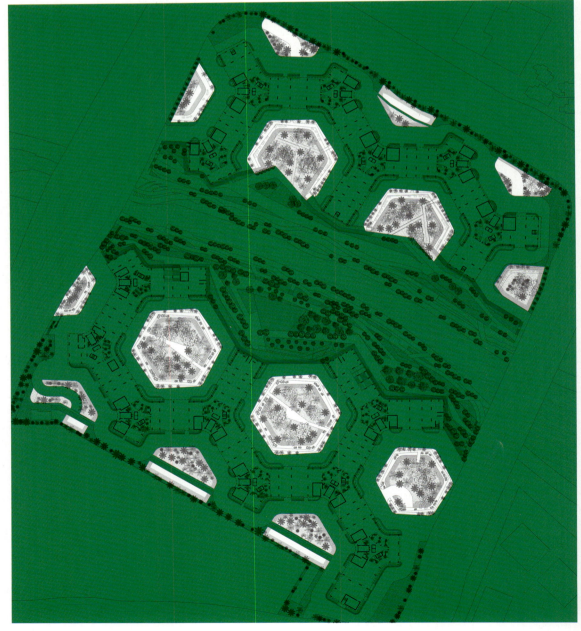

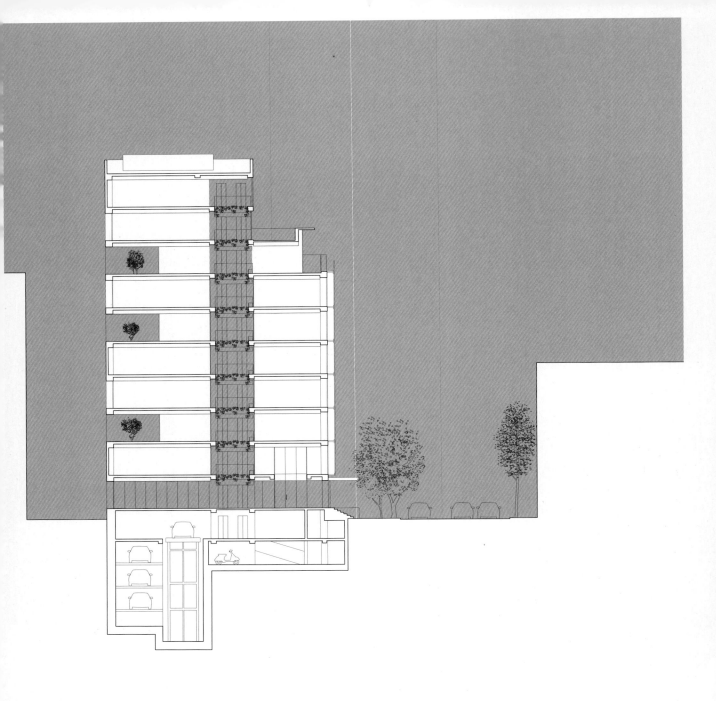
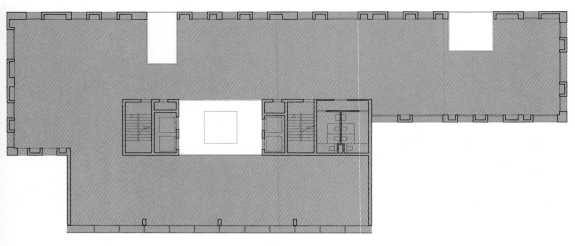

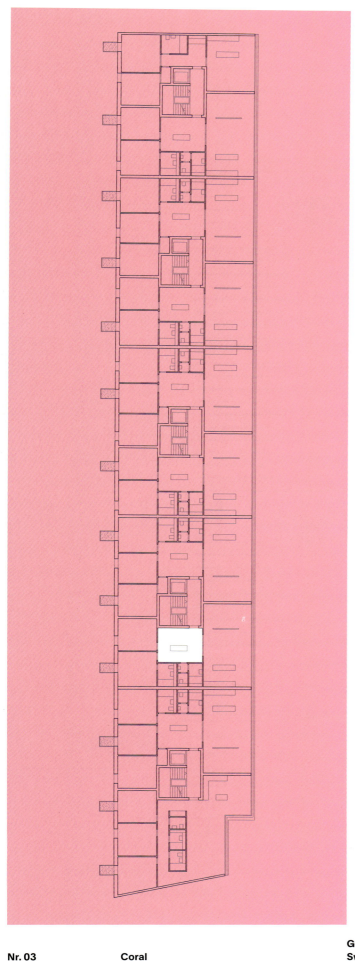

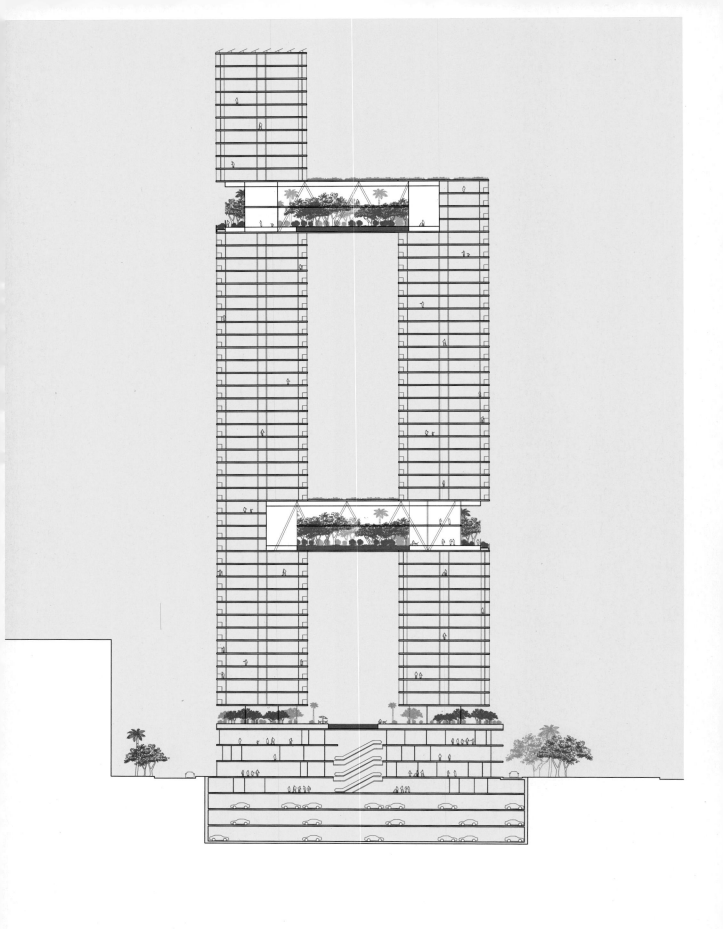

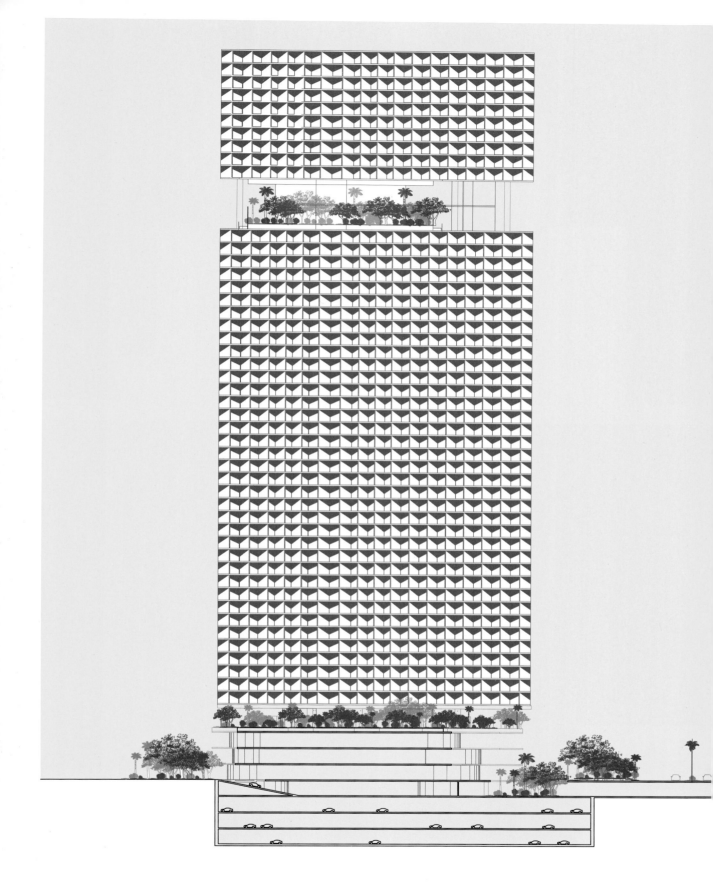

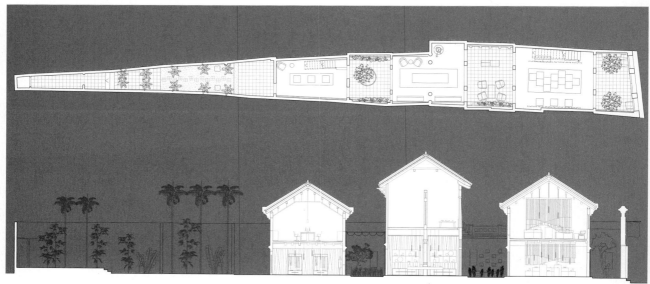

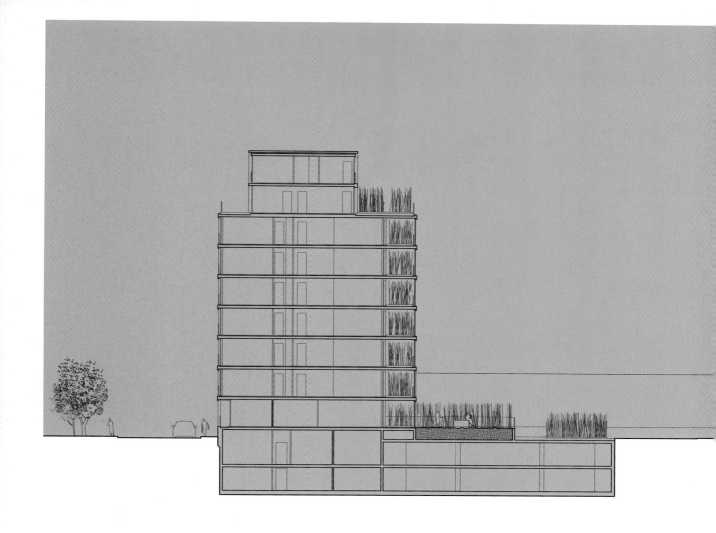

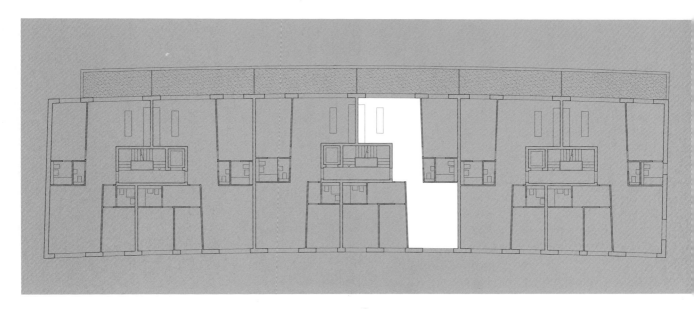

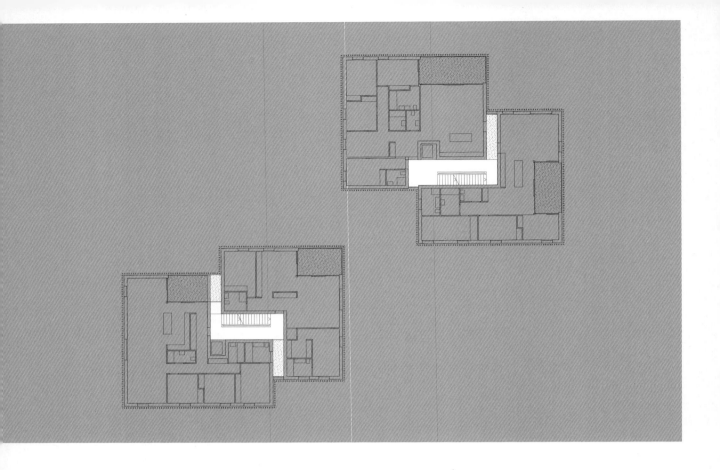

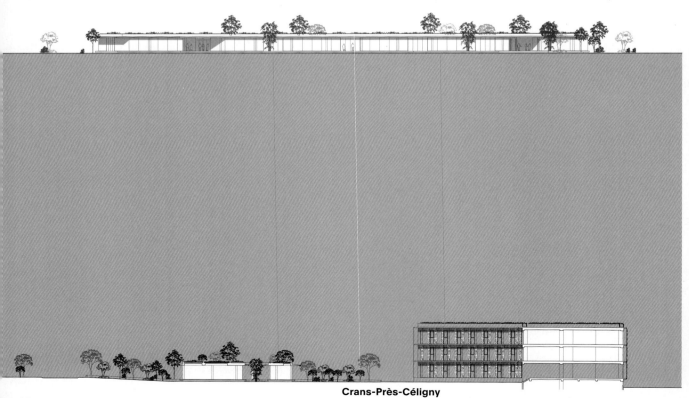

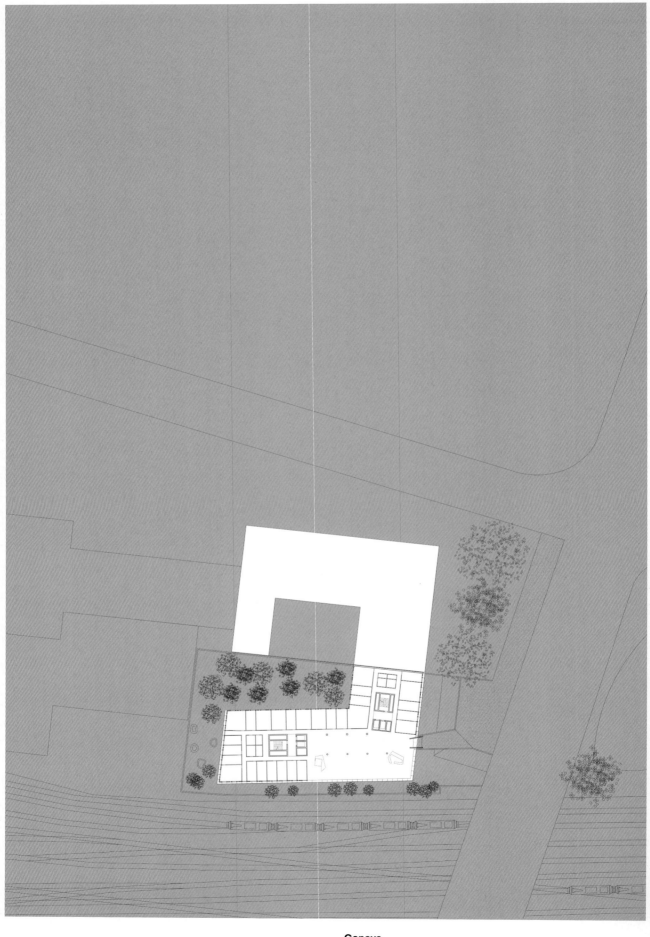

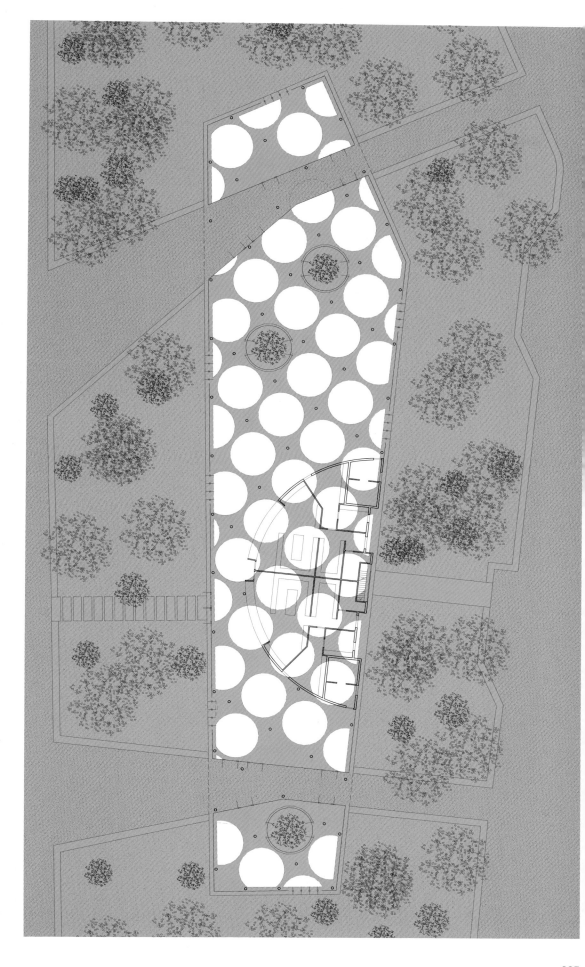

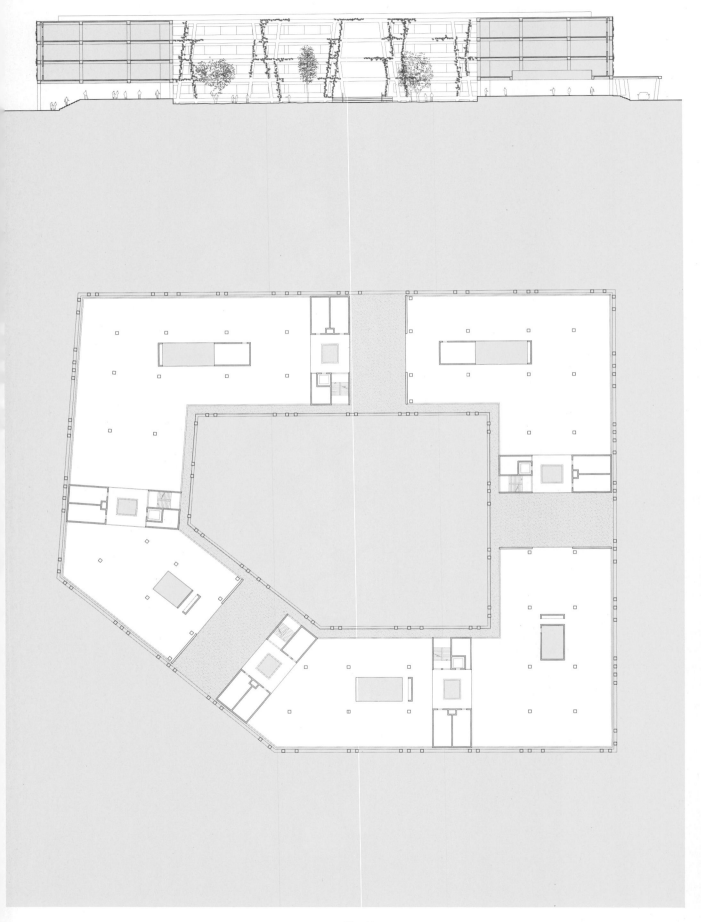

Concrete Lace
The Twin-Lah
Green Dots

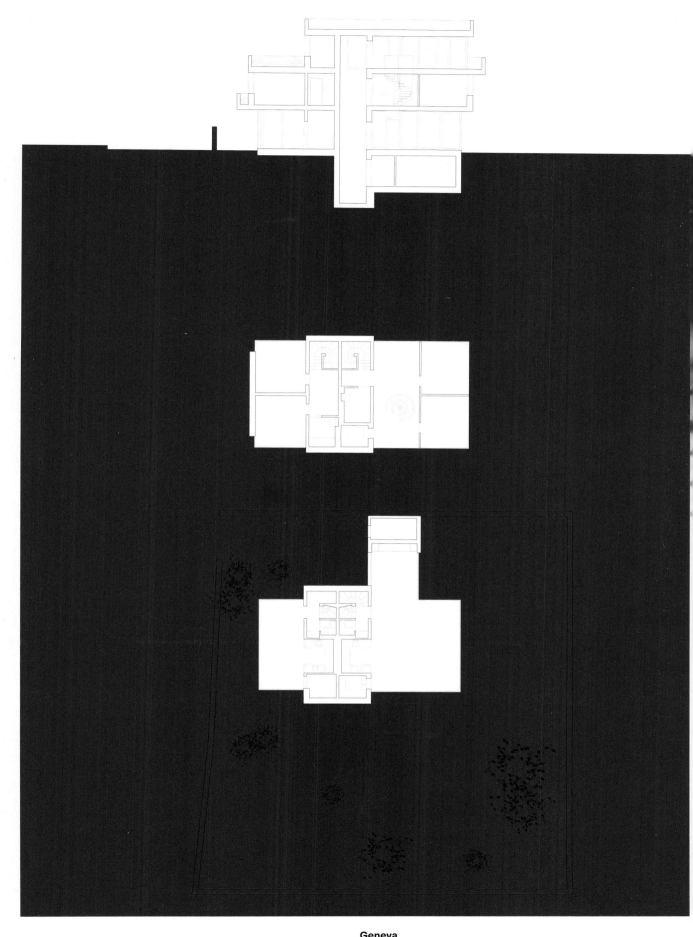

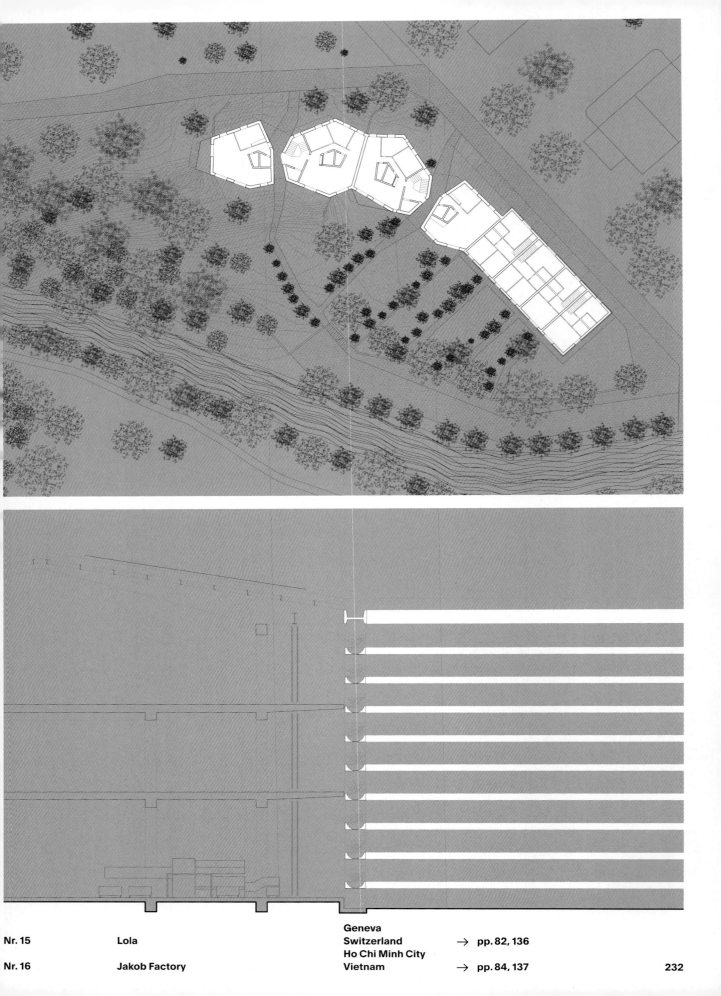

Lola
Jakob Factory
Wood in the Sky
Gordon-Bennett

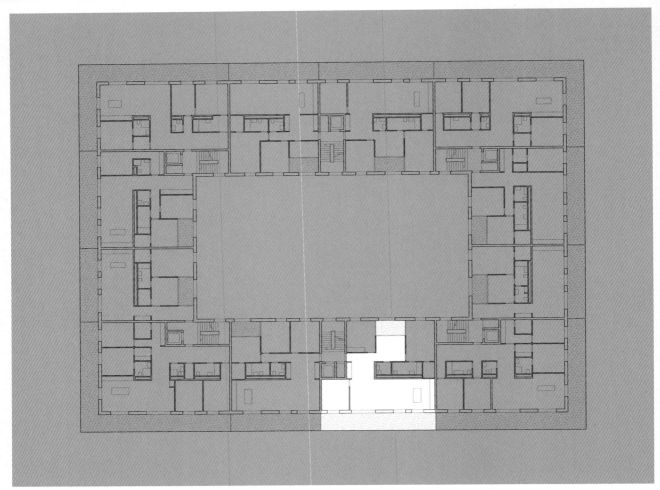

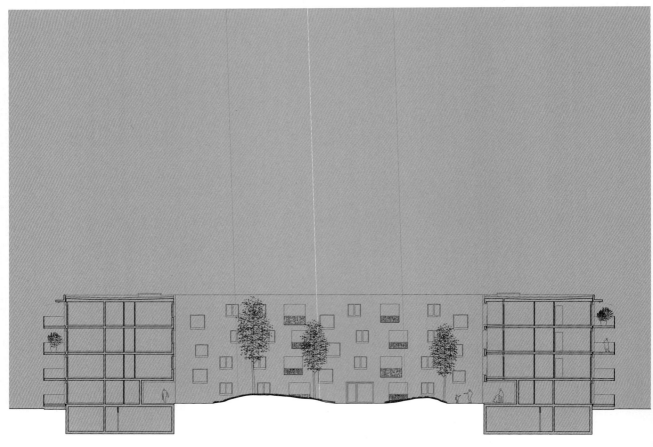

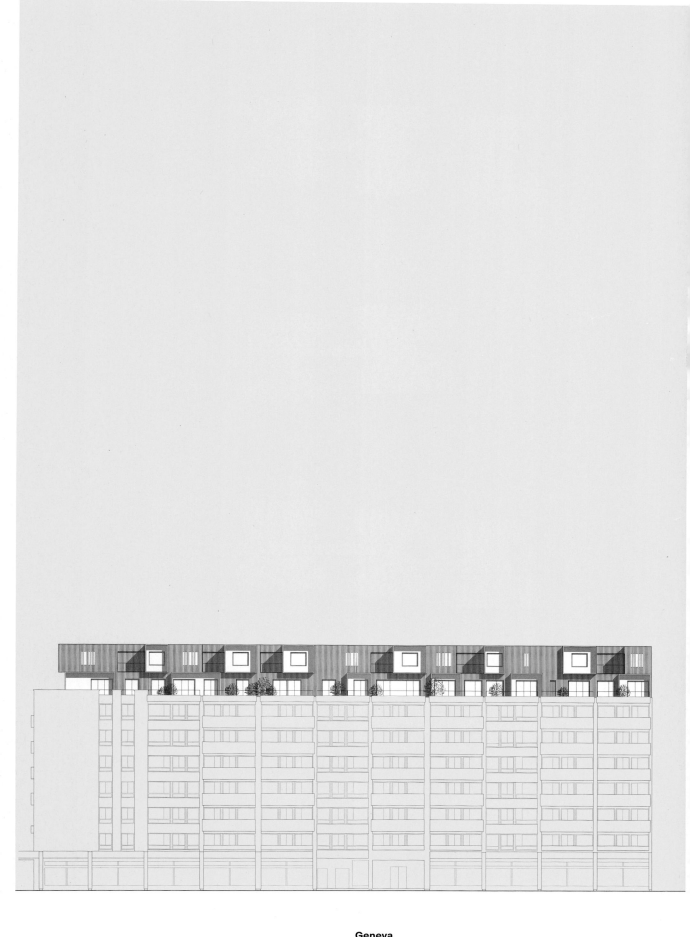

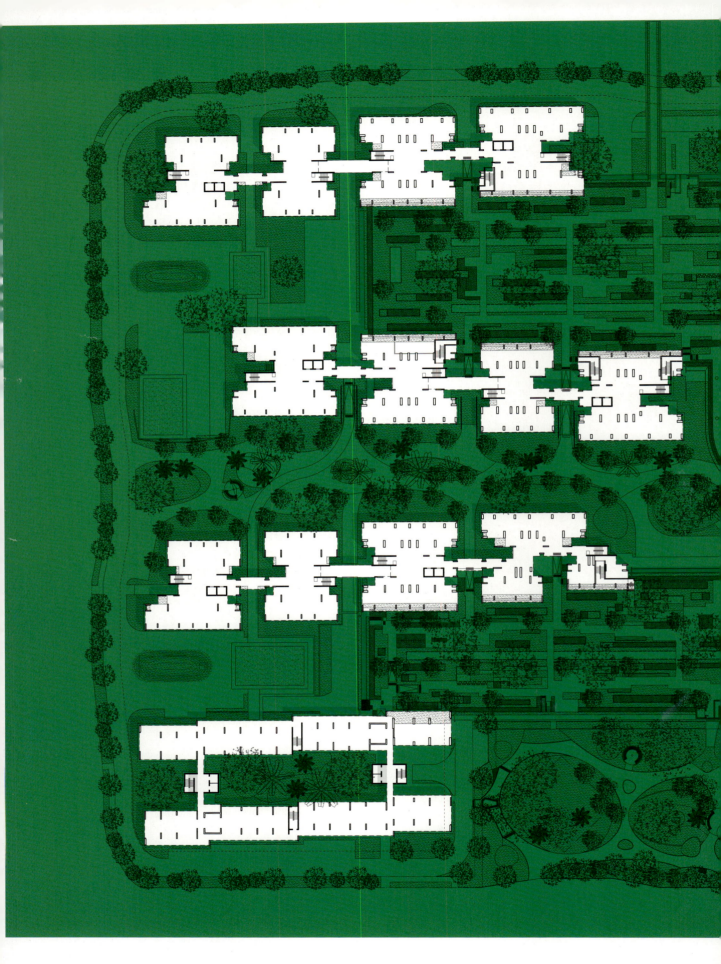

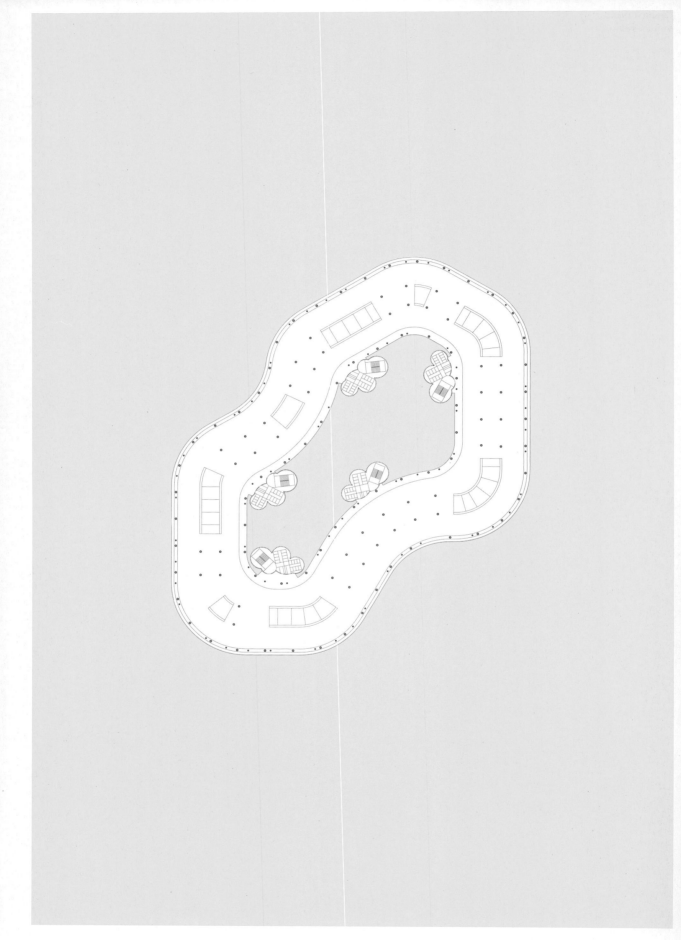

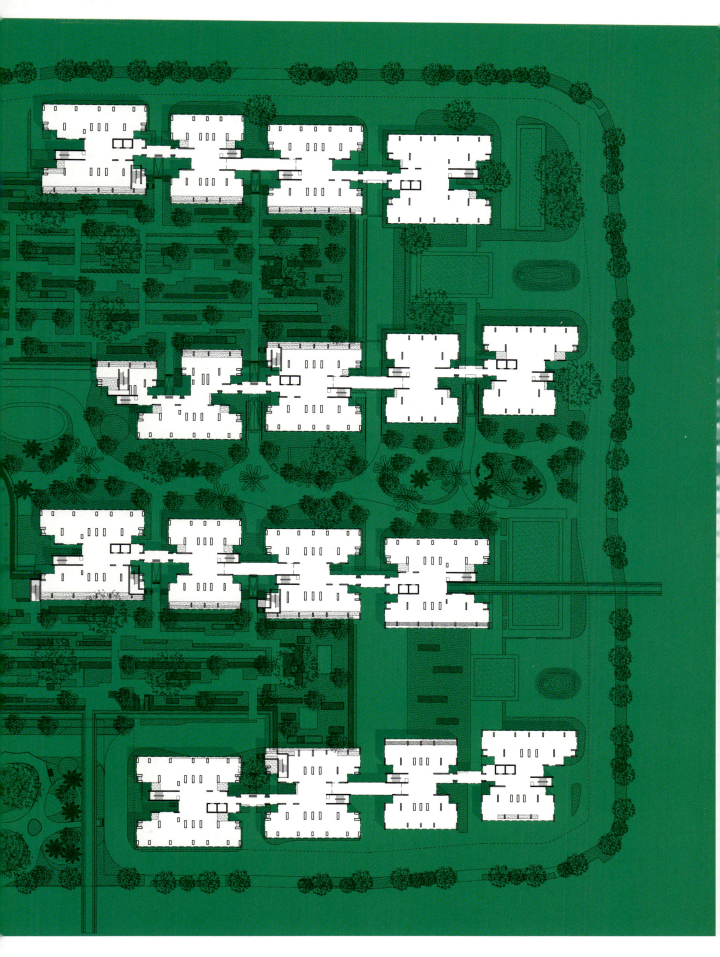

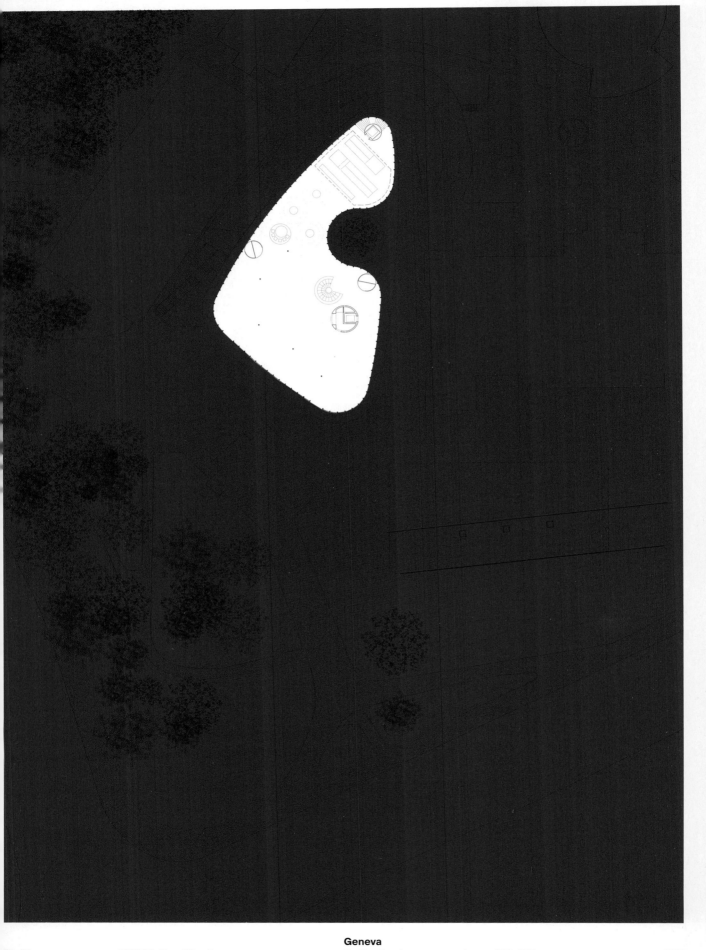

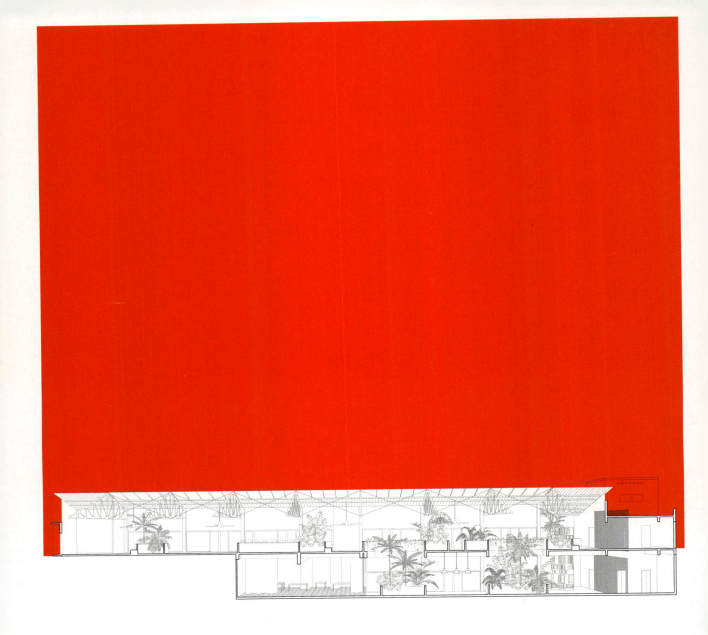

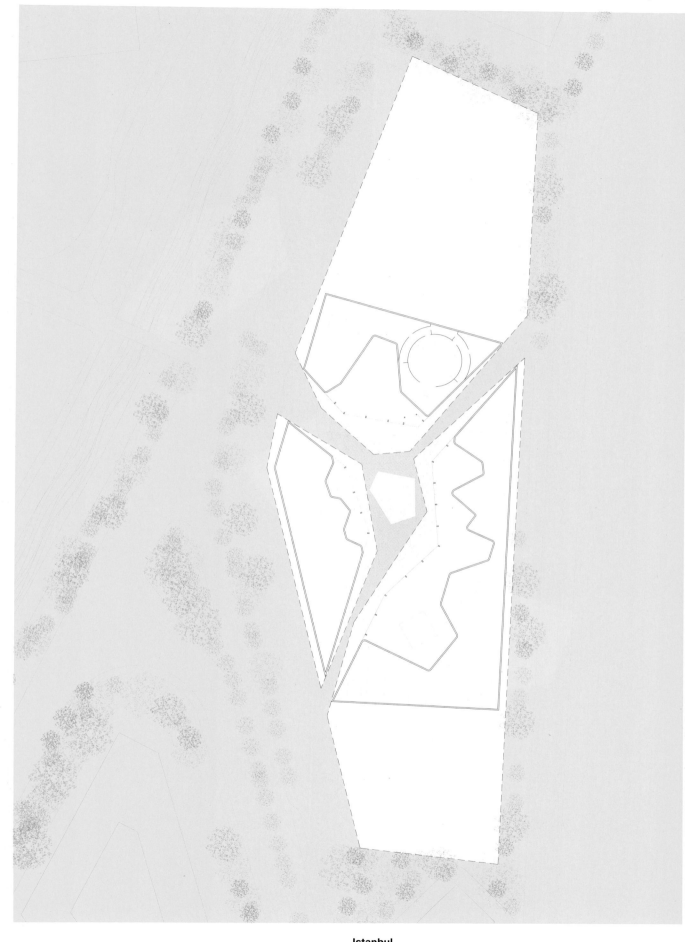

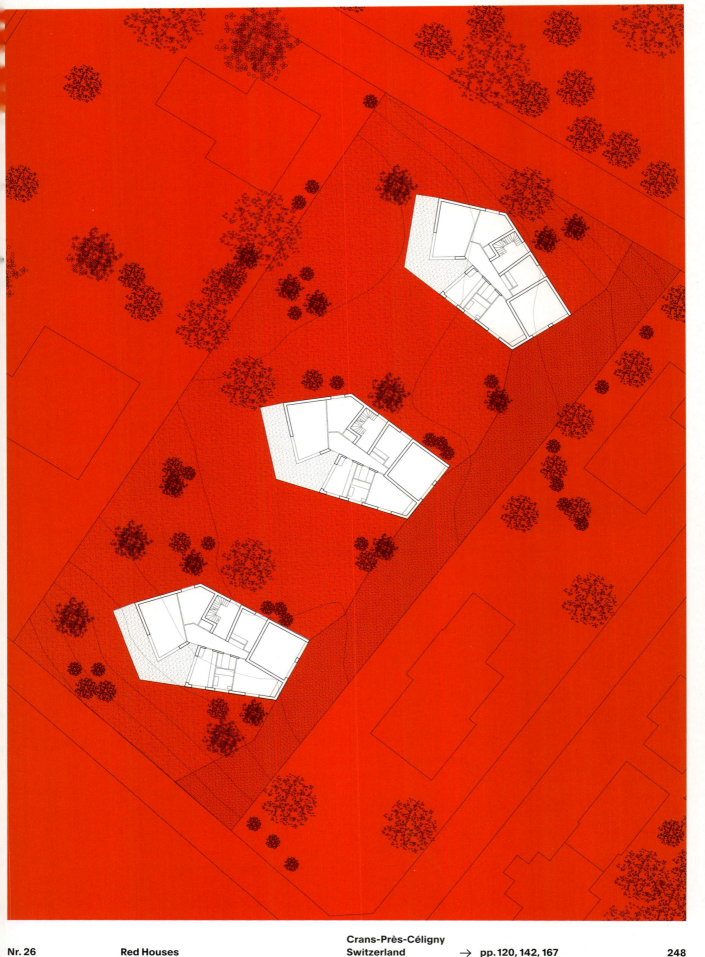

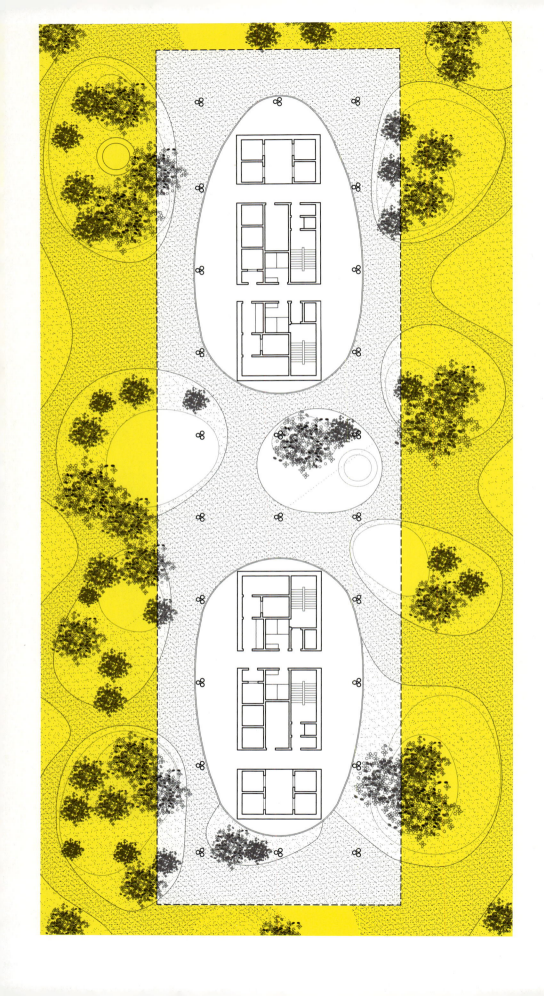

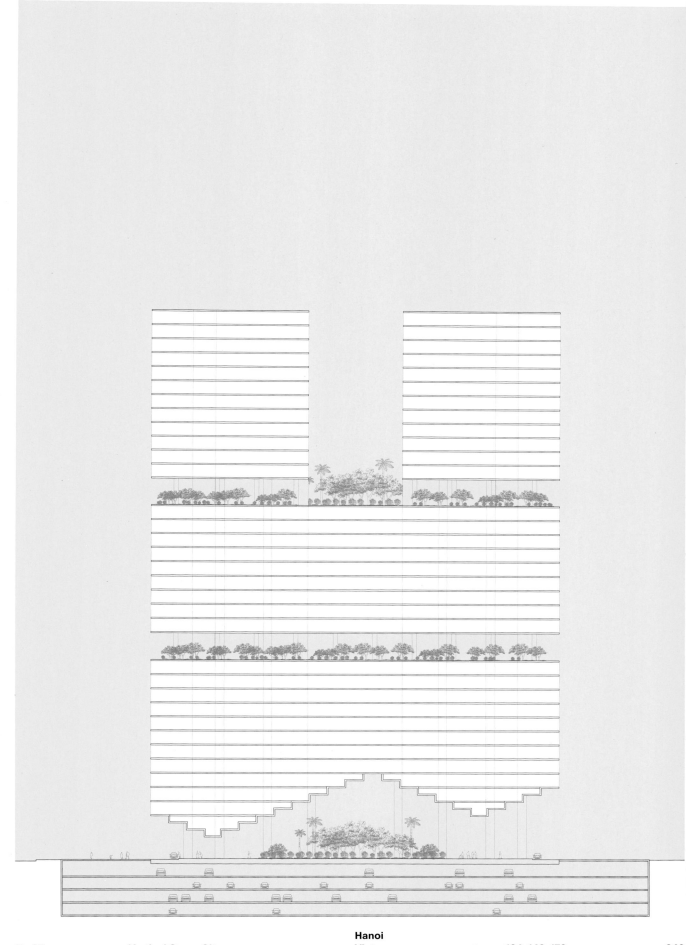

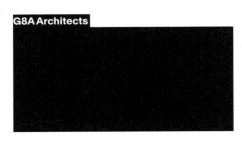

Our architectural journey has been relentlessly optimistic and exhilarating, one which has embraced both the possibilities and the challenges of global practice in the 21st century.

In the year 2000, two Swiss architectural graduates — Manuel Der Hagopian and Grégoire Du Pasquier — joined up with six friends in Geneva to form group8, which was more of an architectural collective than a formal corporate practice. The eight young architects shared their ideas, engaged in debate, contributed to each other's projects, and the fledgling partnership quickly made a name for itself: within a few years group8 became well-known for the hothouse intensity of its creative processes and for the quality of its built projects in the Geneva region.

Der Hagopian and Du Pasquier wanted to broaden their horizons, they had become aware of the increasingly global nature of architectural practice, and they perceived that the constraints of Switzerland's tightly regulated building codes would limit their creative progress. Attracted by the entrepreneurial energy of the emerging property market in Asia, they expanded their operations in order to enjoy the best of both worlds.

In 2007, Der Hagopian and Du Pasquier opened a studio in Hanoi, whilst retaining their collaborative role in the Geneva partnership. As a result of the pair's European experience and newly acquired Asian enthusiasm, the new venture accelerated the trajectory of their architectural expertise. Whilst they were enjoying the critical acclaim that their Swiss projects were receiving, they were now attracting a range of commissions in a completely new environment.

Climatically, culturally, and economically, the rapidly growing cities of Asia were indeed a world away, but the two architects judiciously implemented a strategy of cohesion, which embraced and resolved the perceived contrasts between East and West and between the Old World and the New. As Der Hagopian and Du Pasquier repeatedly declare… "From West to East, we have an ongoing love affair." On the one hand, they brought their Swiss rationality and structural logic to Asia, and on the other they could now consider their European projects with a fresh set of ideas for pragmatic construction and socially responsible design.

The newly formed Hanoi studio was thrust into the limelight with the 2009 competition-winning scheme for Punggol Waterway Terraces in Singapore. Completed in 2015, the project demonstrated a commitment to both environmental sustainability and social cohesion, and it has set a benchmark for large-scale public housing in densely populated Asian cities. The same environmental and social philosophy underpins their ongoing designs for commercial and residential developments throughout Asia, and many of those in Vietnam seek to reinterpret the traditional connections between rural villages and communal life.

A continuing stream of public and semi-public projects in Switzerland have seen a conscientious reassessment and reinvigoration of urban precincts, in both the cities and interconnected villages of a country that is feeling the pressures of increasing densification. As in Asia, a consistent awareness of context and the environment is coupled with community responsibility.

Now known as G8A, the thriving offshoot from the original practice became an independent partnership in 2014. Headed up by Der Hagopian and Du Pasquier with Nicolas Moser and Laurence Savy, G8A has offices in Hanoi, Ho Chi Minh City, Singapore, and Geneva.

A fundamental reason for the success of G8A has been the capacity of the architects to adapt and assimilate their strategies for dissimilar locations: the underlying strengths of their architecture are calibrated for the specific climatic, cultural, and economic demands of such seemingly varied contexts. Singapore is not Hanoi, and Geneva is not Ho Chi Minh City, but the architecture of G8A is immediately identifiable and the factors that determine that architectural signature remain constant.

G8A's designs for Asia reflect an unusually finely-honed eye for detail, their recent work in Europe introduces newly-acquired techniques for practical and efficient construction, and all their architecture demonstrates a passion for creating places that are humanly scaled, culturally vibrant, and environmentally responsible.

Their journey, from the year 2000 into the new millennium, still has a long way to go, but we believe that G8A now leads the way for genuine — carefully considered and deferential — design reciprocity between geopolitically diverse modes of thinking.

Manuel Der Hagopian (born in 1971 in Geneva, Switzerland) graduated from the Geneva Institute of Architecture, Geneva, Switzerland (IAUG) and Belleville School of Architecture, Paris (ENSAPB) in 1998. He is one of the original Partners of group8 architects, established in Geneva in 2000, and is a co-founder and Partner at G8A in charge of operations at the Singapore office. He also co-manages the offices in Geneva, Hanoi, and Ho Chi Minh City. His main responsibilities include design, direction, conceptual design and project management.

Through G8A's think tank, aptly named 8+, he is currently pursuing his strong interest in the consequences of a rapidly growing population's impact on the residential housing situation in South East Asia. Since 2015, he has been a guest professor at SUTD (Singapore University of Technology and Design), where he aims to strengthen the transfer of architectural and design knowledge between Singapore and Switzerland.

Grégoire Du Pasquier (born 1970 in Geneva, Switzerland) is an architect and graduate of the Swiss Federal Institute of Technology, Lausanne, Switzerland (EPFL) in 1995. He is one of the original Partners of group8 architects, established in Geneva in 2000, and is a co-founder and partner at G8A. Prior to opening his own practice, Du Pasquier gained valuable international design and management experience in New York and Paris, working for internationally well-known companies such as Smith-Miller & Hawkinson and Guedot & Chaslin architects.

Currently in charge of operations at the Ho Chi Minh City and Geneva offices, Du Pasquier also co-manages the offices in Hanoi and Singapore. His main responsibilities include design direction, conceptual design, and project management. Du Pasquier is at the head of all development projects across the G8A offices and is the initial contact for potential projects, competitions, and collaborations. He represents the values of G8A in his application of Swiss industry knowledge in the international, and specifically Asian, context. His practice has led him to develop expert knowledge of regional production on all scales of design.

Nicolas Moser (born in 1977 in La Chaux-de-Fonds, Switzerland) graduated from the Swiss Federal Institute of Technology, Lausanne, Switzerland (EPFL) in 2006. He joined group8 architects in Geneva in 2003 and pioneered the strategic move to establish an Asian office later becoming director at G8A in 2015. Moser has been instrumental in the ongoing success of G8A, his main responsibilities include concept design, direction, implementation, and management operations at the Hanoi office.

He supervises G8A's human resources department in South East Asia and has a keen interest in developing projects and contacts in the Republic of Korea and Taiwan. Through experience gained in both Switzerland and Asia, he has a thorough understanding of the cultural and creative processes required by an international design office.

Laurence Savy (born in 1979 in Paris, France) graduated in 2004 from the Architectural School of Paris Malaquais in Paris, France (EAPM) and joined G8A in 2009 becoming a Director in 2015. At G8A, Savy manages operations at the Hanoi office and her responsibilities include design and technical coordination, from conceptual to execution stages for various building types, including residential complexes, corporate offices, educational, institutional, hotel, mixed-use, and retail facilities.

Prior to joining G8A, Savy gained valuable international design experience in Paris, Shanghai, and Geneva. In addition to managing competitions and current projects, she is the communications director, organizer of the Hanoi Talks conferences and is presently engaged in a range of theoretical research.

Project Information

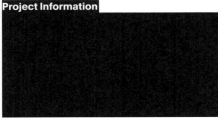

• Projects were completed under the name of group8 where Manuel Der Hagopian and Grégoire Du Pasquier were co-founding members since the inception in the year 2000 and until the recent dissolution of the group.

Punggol Waterway Terraces
Location
Singapore
Program
Housing (1,876 units)
Date
2009–2015
Partner
Aedas
Consultants
Beca Carter Hollings & Ferner (structural & MEP engineering)
Davis Langdon & Seah (quantity surveying)
ICN Design (landscape)
Photographers
Patrick Bingham-Hall
Darren Soh

Coalimex
Location
Hanoi, Vietnam
Program
Office
Date
2008–2013
Partner
VNCC
Photographer
Federal Studio, Régis Golay

Coral •
Location
Geneva, Switzerland
Program
Housing (58 units) / Commercial
Date
2009–2011
Consultants
PBM Planungs und Baumanagement (project management)
Walt+Galmarini
Perreten & Milleret (structural engineering)
SB technique
Mab ingénierie
Mike Humbert (MEP engineering)
Basler & Hoffmann (building engineering physics)
Photographers
Patrick Bingham-Hall
Federal Studio, Régis Golay

The Parks
Location
Quy Nhon, Vietnam
Program
Hotel / Housing / Commercial Center
Date
2016
Consultants
Ney and partners (structure engineering)
Boydens engineering (MEP engineering)
VNCC (local consultant)

The Birds •
Location
Geneva, Switzerland
Program
Birdcage
Date
2007–2008
Consultants
Ingeni (structural engineering)
Photographer
Patrick Bingham-Hall

The Bridge
Location
Hanoi, Vietnam
Program
Office
Date
2016–2019
Partners
Atelier VUUV
Consultants
Jakob Engineering
Photographer
Le Hai Anh

Bamboo •
Location
Geneva, Switzerland
Program
Housing (46 units)
Date
2009–2011
Consultants
PBM Planungs und Baumanagement (project management)
Walt+Galmarini
Perreten & Milleret (structural engineering)
SB technique
Mab ingénierie
Mike Humbert (MEP engineering)
Basler & Hoffmann (building engineering physics)
Photographer
Patrick Bingham-Hall

Hanoia House
Location
Hanoi, Vietnam
Program
Boutique
Date
2016
Photographer
Le Hai Anh

Striped Living •
Location
Crans-près-Céligny, Switzerland
Program
Housing (16 units) / Kindergarten
Date
2007–2012
Consultants
Quartal (project management)
Ingeni (structural engineering)
SB technique
Mab-ingénierie
Zanini-Baechli (MEP engineering)
Photographer
Patrick Bingham-Hall

Hoa Lac High-Tech Park
Location
Hanoi, Vietnam
Program
Office / Multifunctional Pavilion
Date
2010–2015
Consultant
VNC (structural & MEP engineering)
Photographers
Patrick Bingham-Hall
Federal Studio, Régis Golay
Hélène Maria Photographe

Avenue de France •
Location
Geneva, Switzerland
Program
Office
Date
2009–2012
Consultants
Amsler & Bombeli (structural engineering)
Riedweg & Gendre
Mab ingénierie (MEP engineering)
Photographer
Patrick Bingham-Hall

Concrete Lace
Location
Hanoi, Vietnam
Program
Office
Date
2014–2016
Consultant
CDC (structural & MEP engineering)
Photographers
Patrick Bingham-Hall
Le Hai Anh

The Twin-Lah
Location
Geneva, Switzerland
Program
Housing
Date
2016–2019
Partners
Collin Fontaine
Consultants
Ingeni (structural enginnering)
Photographer
Federal Studio, Régis Golay

Green Dots
Location
Seoul, Republic of Korea
Program
Public Facilities / Public Spaces / Theatre /
    Landscape
Date
2016
Consultants
Ney + partners (structural engineering)
Boydens engineering (MEP engineering)
Nam Sung-Taeg (local consultant,
    Hanyang University)

Lola •
Location
Geneva, Switzerland
Program
Housing (14 units)
Date
2009–2013
Consultants
Amsler & Bombeli (structural engineering)
SB technique (MEP engineering)
Photographer
Patrick Bingham-Hall

Jakob Factory
Location
Ho Chi Minh City, Vietnam
Program
Factory / Office / Facilities
Date
2015–2019
Partner
Rollimarchini
Consultants
Archetype Group
NKC (structural & MEP engineering)
Artelia (project manager)
Photographer
Quang Dam

Wood in the Sky •
Location
Geneva, Switzerland
Program
Housing (6 units)
Date
2009–2012
Consultants
Beric (general contractor)
EDMS (structural engineering)
Photographer
Patrick Bingham-Hall

Gordon Bennett •
Location
Geneva, Switzerland
Program
Housing (44 units)
Date
2007–2013
Consultants
LRS architectes (master planning)
CSD engineers (structural engineering)
Mab-ingénierie
Perrin & Spaeth
Schumacher ingénierie (MEP engineering)
Photographers
Patrick Bingham-Hall
Federal Studio, Régis Golay

Green Ridges
Location
Singapore
Program
Housing (2,000 units)
Date
2013–2018
Partner
Laud Architects
Consultants
Beca Carter Hollings & Ferner (structural
    & MEP engineering)
Davis Langdon & Seah (quantity surveying)
ICN Design (landscape)
Photographers
Patrick Bingham-Hall
Studio Periphery

Infinity Village
Location
Hanoi, Vietnam
Program
Office / Facilities
Date
2017–2021
Consultant
NDC

ICRC Visitor Centre •
Location
Geneva, Switzerland
Program
Office / Conference Rooms / Exhibition /
    Restaurant
Date
2009–2014
Consultants
EDMS (structural engineering)
Zanetti (MEP engineering)
Photographer
Patrick Bingham-Hall

Jungle Station
Location
Ho Chi Minh City, Vietnam
Program
Office / Co-working space
Date
2017–2018
Photographer
Quang Dam

La Tuilerie •
Location
Geneva, Switzerland
Program
Housing (25 units)
Date
2008–2012
Partner
Atelier d'Architecture Jacques Bugna
Consultants
Amsler & Bombeli (structural engineering)
Mike Humbert
Scherler (MEP engineering)
Photographer
Federal Studio, Régis Golay

Epicentre

Location
Istanbul, Turkey
Program
**Education Center / Exhibition Hall /
    Planetarium / Conference Centre /
    Office**
Date
2011

Oerlikon

Location
Zurich, Switzerland
Program
Office / Housing / Public Space
Date
2013–2016
Consultants
Kaufman (project management)
Franz Bitterli (structural engineering)
SBT (MEP engineering)
**Basler & Hofmann
    (building engineering physics)**
Photographer
Federal Studio, Régis Golay

Red Houses •

Location
Crans-près-Céligny, Switzerland
Program
Housing (6 units)
Date
2006–2008
Consultants
Ingeni (structural engineering)
SB technique (MEP engineering)
Photographer
DGBP David Gagnebin-de Bons Benoît Pointet

Vertical Green City

Location
Hanoi, Vietnam
Program
**Office / Housing / Facilities /
    Commercial Centre**
Date
2016
Partner
VNCC

Partners & Directors

Manuel Der Hagopian
Grégoire Du Pasquier
Nicolas Moser
Laurence Savy

Current Staff

Andrea Archanco Astorga
Mathieu Boucachard
Axel Bouffart
Thi Linh Bui
Megha Chamaria
Pierre-Eloi Coste
Martial Coudamy
Ramon Cuesta Conzales de la Aleja
Armand Devillard
Quoc Hoan Do
Hiep Thuong Duong
Bao Trung Duong
Miguel Guevara
Quang Anh Ha
Johannes Hansen
Marine Jombart
Samia Kenley
Amber Kevelaerts
Nhat Truong Son Khuc
Ravish Kumar
Hai Anh Le
Hoang Linh Le
Ngoc Toan Le
Hai Ly Le
Quang Le
Elise Luong
Francesco Montresor
Duy Tan Nguyen
Phuong Thao Nguyen
Hung Son Nguyen
Nhat Linh Nguyen
Van Thanh Nguyen
Duy Thanh Nguyen
Ha Mau Lien Nguyen
Thuy Tien Nguyen
Quynh Tram Ninh
Kousuke Osawa
Thanh Chung Pham
Viet Anh Pham
Tran Hoang Pham
Quoc Huy Pham
Thanh Nam Pham
Hoai Thanh Phan
The Ngoc Phan
Alexia Roziecki
Julio Rufian Andujar
Mathilde Ruiz
Sopheap Sok
Thi Minh Ha Tran
Van Hung Tran
Paul Trellu
Quynh Le Trinh
Thu Linh Vu

Acknowledgements

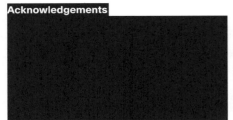

Over the past decades, G8A has witnessed many changes in organization, geography, development, and projects. Through these years, we have had the chance to work with a great variety of individuals, all contributing their specific talent to our projects. We would like to sincerely thank all those past and present who have worked as part of our team and made G8A what it is today.

This publication is born specifically from the hard work of a group of creatives that we would like to thank for their vision, dedication and enthusiasm

Elise Luong
Jonas Voegeli
Laurence Savy
Nicolas Moser
Patrick Bingham-Hall
Regis Golay
Scott Vander Zee

Many of our projects are the result of successful collaborations and we are lucky to have beside us our partners

Blaise Fontaine
Didier Collin
Jason Bok
Joseph Lau
Ho Tzu Yin
Hoe Theong
Kurt Aellen
Le Cuong
Melvin Tan
Michel Rolli
Ngo Trunh Hai
Nguyen Ba Hung
Nguyen Trung Dung
Phan Minh Son
Tony Ang
Tran Binh Trọng
Tran Vu Lam
Vu Hoang Ha

A final thank you to our partners from former group8, with whom we have shared an extraordinary adventure for over ten years

Adrien Besson
Christophe Pidoux
Daniel Zamarbide
François de Marignac
Laurent Ammeter
Oscar Frisk
Tarramo Broennimann

Imprint

Edited by
G8A Architects

Texts
Patrick Bingham-Hall

Proofreading
Anna Roos

Photography / Renderings
Patrick Bingham-Hall
pp. 15–20, 22–23, 37–38, 43–47, 50–53, 56–59, 61 (bottom), 63, 65, 68–74, 82–83, 86–91, 95, 100–105
Federal Studio, Régis Golay
pp. 25–36, 60, 61 (top), 62, 78–79, 92–93, 110–113, 117–119
Darren Soh
p. 21
Quang Dam
pp. 84, 107–109
Studio Periphery
pp. 96–97
Le Hai Anh
pp. 48–49, 54–55, 75–77
DGBP David Gagnebin-de Bons Benoît Pointet
pp. 120–123
Hélène Maria Photographe
pp. 64, 66–67
G8A Architects
pp. 40–41, 80–81, 85, 99, 114–115, 124–125

Graphic design
Jonas Voegeli
Scott Vander Zee
(Hubertus Design)

Lithography
Marjeta Morinc

Printing and binding
Musumeci S.p.A

Paper
Munken Polar Rough 100 g/m²
Terra Print Gloss 90 g/m²
Prolight 50 g/m²

Typeface
Plain by François Rappo
optimo.ch

Park Books
Niederdorfstrasse 54
8001 Zurich
Switzerland
park-books.com

Park Books is being supported by the Federal Office of Culture with a general subsidy for the years 2016–2020.